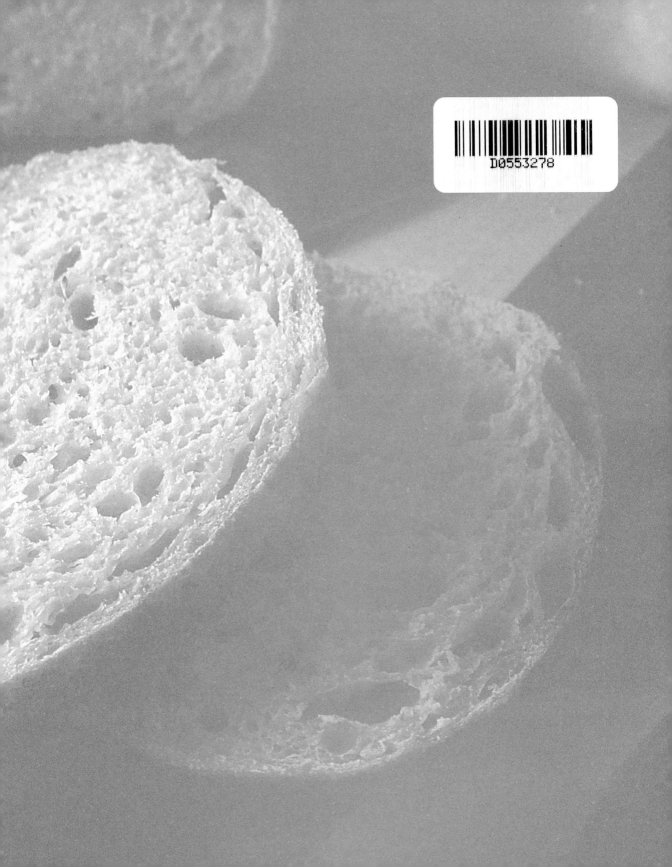

D0553278

BREAD

BREAD

Simple and satisfying recipes
for the bread machine.

Kathryn
Hawkins

NEW
HOLLAND

CONTENTS

Introduction   6

Ingredients for bread making   10

Bread machine basics   18

Bread machine golden rules   21

Handy hints   23

Troubleshooting   26

Loaves   28

Doughs   98

Cakes and tea breads   130

Serving suggestions   150

Accompaniments   170

Bibliography   178

About the author   179

Index   180

Introduction

Thanks to bread machines, gone are the long hours of dough preparation: kneading, proving, re-kneading, rising and then baking. Once you've measured out the ingredients, all you have to do is set the programme and leave the rest to the machine.

If you're concerned about what goes into the food you eat, making your own bread enables you to control the quality of the ingredients that go into this daily staple, and you can make and adapt recipes to suit your personal tastes and preferences – great if you're on a restricted diet. And, what's more, the family will love the homely smells of freshly baking bread wafting from the kitchen.

In this book, I explain the principles involved in using a bread machine (whatever the make and model, the principles are the same) and the most important factors necessary for attaining the perfect result.

I explain the different programme settings, to help you choose the correct cycle for your bread, and include a valuable troubleshooting guide to help you if things go wrong. You'll also find information on different flours, yeast and other ingredients you can use in your baking. It is very important that you read all of these sections before you start making your own bread.

Once you've read through the introductory pages, you'll be looking forward to getting started. The first few recipes in the Loaves chapter (see pages 30–51) are straightforward breads to help boost your bread-making confidence. Once you've mastered these, move on to the rest of the recipes in this chapter and start experimenting with different flavours and textures.

The shape, size, flavour, texture and colour of

bread has developed over time, and we have become increasingly experimental, using the different types of grain and a wealth of exotic ingredients that are available to us today. Because of increasing demands on our busy everyday lives, we no longer have the time to bake our own bread conventionally at home, relying instead on professional bakers to provide us with our daily loaf. In recent years, however, the most important development in bread making has been the increase in popularity of the domestic bread machine.

At the end of the nineteenth century an American inventor developed a machine that mixed and kneaded bread dough at speed, but it took a further 100 years for the Japanese to pick up on the idea and develop a machine able to process the whole loaf from start to finish. These machines became very popular in the United States; no longer were housewives dependent on a good baker or local grocery store for their daily supply of bread, but could make their own bread at home with the minimum of fuss and effort.

Europeans were initially a little less enthusiastic about welcoming yet another gadget on to their already crowded kitchen worktops, and it wasn't until the late 1990s that using a bread machine really took off.

PRINCIPLES OF BREAD MAKING

Bread is made from a flour and water dough, fermented with yeast, which is then kneaded and baked. The main reason bread evolved is because finely ground grains such as wheat, barley or rye are not easy to digest on their own; mixing the flour into a paste or dough with liquid and cooking it, however, renders it palatable.

The main use of flour through the ages has been to make bread. Wheat and rye are the only two cereals that have the unique property of forming gluten. Gluten is a protein which absorbs water and forms a stringy network within a dough once it is mixed and kneaded; it is the gluten that gives bread its elasticity. This explains why loaves made with other types of flour or the specially prepared gluten-free flours have a heavy, more cake-like texture.

When you add yeast to the mix you are able to refine the dough from a tough, pasty structure to a lighter, softer one. This happens because yeast is a living organism and given the right conditions – warmth, food and water – it produces carbon dioxide. This gas helps the glutenous strands to expand, pushing them out and trapping bubbles in the web-like network. Once the bread is put in the oven, the heat sets the structure, the trapped gases escape and the familiar loaf-like structure is formed and baked rigid.

INGREDIENTS FOR BREAD MAKING

Before you start using your bread machine, it is important to have a basic understanding about the ingredients that are suitable for bread making and the results you can expect from using them.

Flours

Wheat-based flours

Wheat flours with a high protein content, 10.5% or more, will make the best bread. Below are the different types of wheat flour I have used:

Plain white flour

Traditional multi-purpose, plain white flour is milled from soft wheat grains and contains around 9.5–10% protein and consequently doesn't contain enough gluten to make a good bread dough. The bran and germ are removed during processing and the flour is made from the starchy white centre called endosperm. Plain white flour is best for making pastries, cakes and tea breads, when raising agents other than yeast are used and a light, spongy texture is required. Sometimes plain white flour can be mixed with stronger-protein wheat flour to give a closer textured loaf.

White bread flour

Also called strong and very strong white bread flour, it is milled from hard wheat grains that have a higher protein level. The protein content can range from 12–14%, depending on the manufacturer, which makes it much more suitable for bread making.

Plain wholemeal flour

Contains all the wheat grain (bran and germ) and so is more nutritious than white flours as it has a higher fibre content. As with plain white flour, use this flour for pastries, cakes and tea breads only, as the protein content isn't high enough for bread making.

Wholemeal bread flour

Also called strong wholemeal bread flour. Choose a flour with a protein content of around 12.5%

for bread making. Loaves made with 100% wholemeal bread flour can have a denser, heavier texture because the bran content inhibits the gluten development. Therefore, for a lighter loaf, you might want to mix it with varying proportions of white bread flour depending on the desired result.

Soft-grain strong white bread flour

Strong white bread flour with added kibbled or "cracked" wheat and rye grains, which add texture. It has a higher fibre content than white bread flour without the "heaviness" of 100% wholemeal. For this reason, it is a good halfway measure in a battle to get the kids to eat more fibre!

Granary® malted brown bread flour

Also called country grain, malted wheatgrain and malthouse flour. This is a strong wheat flour with around 14% protein content. It has malted wheat flakes added to it, which give it a higher nutritive value and a nutty, slightly sweet flavour.

Spelt flour

A flour made from an ancient wheat grain, Triticum spelta, used in Roman times. The grain is milled to give a light wholemeal flour, which has a lower gluten content than other wheat flours. For this reason, it makes a cakier textured loaf when used on its own. It has a delicious flavour, and is most successful when mixed with white bread flour. The type of gluten found in spelt flour is easier to digest, and can sometimes be tolerated by people with a wheat gluten allergy.

NOTE: Always check with your GP first, though, if you do have such an allergy.

Other grain flours

Buckwheat

Also known as beechwheat, brank, or Saracen corn, buckwheat is a plant related to rhubarb. Its triangular-shaped kernels are greyish in colour, gluten-free and a natural source of rutin, which is used as a natural remedy for circulatory problems; it is also a good source of calcium and protein. The kernels are milled to make a flour which gives a fragrant, nutty flavour. Because there is no gluten in buckwheat, it is usually mixed with wheat flour in bread making.

Rye

Has been widely used in bread making since Roman times and it grows well in cold, wet climates not tolerated by wheat, hence its popularity in the cooking of northeastern Europe, Scandinavia and Russia. It does contain some gluten and when used on its own produces a very dense and heavy bread, so it is better mixed with white or wholemeal bread flours to give a more acceptable texture. Rye flour adds a very slight acidic taste to a bread or cake mix.

Gram

Also called chickpea, garbanzo bean or besan flour. It is made from grinding chickpeas into a fine flour. (Strictly speaking besan flour is made not from chickpeas but from yellow split peas or chana dhal.) It is pale yellow and powdery, and has a beany, earthy flavour, which is more suited to savoury dishes. It contains no gluten and is used in Indian cookery for binding together savoury breads like chapatis and in making dumplings and fritters such as onion bhajis. Best mixed with white bread flour. Available from Asian grocers and health food shops.

Potato

A very starchy, white powdery flour made from potatoes. It contains no gluten and is used in small amounts in conjunction with specific bread flour to lighten and soften a loaf.

Soya

Milled from soybeans, this flour has a very high protein content. It contains no gluten, is low in carbohydrate and is used to enrich the nutritional content of bread flours and give a softer, creamier textured loaf.

Cornmeal

Widely used as a staple in corn-growing parts of the world for both human and animal consumption, it is available in a variety of textures ranging from the very fine to coarser textures sold as polenta. Golden yellow in colour, it has a slightly gritty texture and contains no gluten. It can be used in conjunction with other non-glutenous flours to make dense textured soda-style breads, or with bread flours to give colour and texture.

Rice

Available in white and brown forms. It is starchy, slightly sweet in flavour and the brown variety gives a loaf an element of nuttiness. It is used in small amounts to lighten and soften the bread's crumb.

Gluten-free bread flour

Available in white and brown forms, it is a combination of gluten-free flours such as rice, maize, buckwheat, carob, potato and tapioca, with added natural (xanthan) gum specifically developed for both conventional and machine bread making. Bread made with this flour isn't the same as traditional wheat bread, and recipes are altered accordingly, but it is a good alternative if you are unable to tolerate gluten. The texture is denser and the finish is often less risen and less crusty than other loaves. Available from health food shops.

Yeast

The type of yeast suitable for using in a bread machine is the instant or fast-acting (easy blend) dried yeast that is readily available in the supermarket. Only this type of yeast can be used. This yeast is specially formulated so that it doesn't need to be activated before use and has added ascorbic acid (vitamin C), which increases the strength of the gluten and thus enables a better rise.

The yeast is mostly packaged in small sachets containing about 2½ tsp or 7g. Once opened the yeast doesn't keep long, so seal the sachet carefully and keep in the fridge for up to 48 hours; after this time, its fermenting powers are greatly reduced or lost altogether. The yeast should be mixed into the dry ingredients before it comes into contact with the liquid, and it should be kept away from the salt and sugar (see page 24).

Sourdough starter

This can be made in different ways and is one of the most natural ways to make bread rise and develop texture and flavour. It is a lengthier process, but once a starter is made, it can be replenished, providing you with a continuous supply for your bread making. Flour and water are the basic ingredients, with other things added to encourage fermentation such as honey, soured milk, yogurt and yeast. Bread made using the sourdough method has a slightly acidic flavour and a much more aerated texture. I have included a yeast-fermented starter here for you to experiment with:

500g (1lb) strong white bread flour
4 tsp instant or fast-acting
dried yeast
600ml (20fl oz) water

Mix the flour and yeast together in a large mixing bowl and gradually blend in the water. Cover with a clean tea towel or piece of muslin. Stand at room temperature – ideally in a coolish place, out of sunlight – and leave undisturbed for 3–5 days to ferment. The batter is ready when it is frothy and has a pleasant sour smell. Cover with clingfilm and store in the fridge.

Before using, stand at room temperature for about 30 minutes, and then stir the batter.

Once you have used some of your starter, you will need to replenish it. Providing you do this every two weeks, the starter will keep indefinitely. All you have to do is add the quantity of water/flour that you take out: for example if you need to use 300ml (10fl oz) of the starter, replace it by adding 150ml (5fl oz) water and 125g (4oz) strong white bread flour to the remaining starter. Allow to ferment at room temperature for 24 hours before storing in the fridge once more. This should become an ongoing process to enable you to make a sourdough loaf whenever you want.

Other raising agents

If you want to avoid using yeast in your diet, you can still make bread in your bread machine in the form of soda breads, cakes or tea breads. Usually you will mix the ingredients together prior to putting them into the bread machine pan and cooking on the "bake only" setting.

Baking powder

Baking powder is a mixture of alkaline and acid substances which, when moistened, react to create carbon dioxide gas. This produces a "rise". Commercially-made powder contains bicarbonate of soda (alkaline) and tartaric acid with a dried starch or flour which absorbs any moisture during storage. Make your own by combining 1 Tbsp bicarbonate of soda with 2 Tbsp cream of tartar. Always measure carefully as too much or too little can upset the balance of the recipe. Use this type of mixture quickly to capture the air in the finished loaf.

Bicarbonate of soda

Bicarbonate of soda is an alkaline raising agent used in recipes that contain an acid ingredient such as buttermilk or lemon. It produces carbon dioxide gas when mixed with liquid and should be added just before cooking otherwise the gas will be lost.

Liquid

Water is the most widely used liquid in bread making. NOTE: You should read your own bread machine instructions manual to see whether your machine requires cold or warmed liquid, and follow these instructions carefully. When the bread is being prepared on a quick or rapid setting, the liquid is usually warmed. Fruit and vegetable juices can be used successfully, but often the added sugar quantity is reduced to compensate for the natural sugars in the juice. Liquid milk can be used

– skimmed and semi-skimmed varieties work best, as full-cream milk will give a much closer, more cake-like texture. Coconut milk can be used, and added fat is not necessary because of the high fat content of the coconut. Soya milk also works well for a dairy-free diet.

Sugar

Most bread recipes contain a little sugar in the form of crystalline sugars, honey, syrups, malt extract, treacle or molasses. Measure the quantity stated carefully as adding too much will stop the yeast working to its full capacity, and the rise will not develop. Some bread machines have a sweet bread setting for use with bread mixes that are non-savoury and have increased sugar quantities – these types of bread may brown more than less sweet mixes. This setting is designed to cook the bread more quickly or at a lower temperature to prevent over-browning. If your machine doesn't have this setting, you may want to experiment using a lighter crust setting.

NOTE: All the sweet bread recipes in this book were tested using a normal white bread setting and a satisfactory result was achieved, but since different types of bread machine will differ in usage and performance, you may want to experiment with your own sweet bread setting. Always refer to your bread machine instructions manual and follow the manufacturer's instructions.

Salt

Salt is used to bring out the flavour in a recipe. In bread making, the salt also acts as a brake mechanism, preventing the yeast from over-working and collapsing. Measure out carefully, as adding too much will stop the yeast working altogether. Use natural sea salts rather than salt substitutes.

Fat

A small amount of fat is added to most breads to improve the texture and flavour. Unsalted butter and margarine (to prevent over-seasoning and inhibiting the yeast action), lard, white vegetable fat and vegetable oils are all suitable. Reduced-fat spreads are best avoided because of their higher water content.

Additional ingredients

Dairy products

You can enrich a loaf of bread by replacing some of the water with natural yogurt, evaporated milk, buttermilk, soft cheese such as fromage frais, cottage cheese and mascarpone, or even a small amount of single or unwhipped double cream. The loaf will be more close-textured, and often more moist.

Grated cheese

This can be added to breads at the beginning of the bread making process so it can be thoroughly incorporated and give a lovely savoury flavour. If you add it towards the end of the kneading cycle, distinct pieces of cheese will be seen in the finished loaf. It can also be sprinkled on top just before baking to give a cheesy topping. For a good cheesy flavour, choose small amounts of strong-flavoured cheeses such as Parmesan, mature

Cheddar, Roquefort or Stilton. If the cheese is very salty, like Danish Blue, you will need to reduce the amount of salt that you add in order to get a good rise. Using too much cheese in a dough will prevent the bread from rising well, so weigh out accurately.

Eggs

Eggs can be used to increase the nutritional value of a loaf, and give a creamy colour and rich texture. Choose free-range or organic for the best quality and flavour. Use eggs at room temperature. Beat in a measuring jug before using so that you can top up easily with liquid to the quantity required in the recipe. Adding eggs as well as the full liquid quantity will result in too soft a dough and a poor result.

Skimmed milk powder

Many recipes include this as a standard addition as it improves the crustiness of the finished loaf and adds extra nutritional value. I prefer not to add milk powder to many of my recipes, however, as I think the texture becomes less bread-like if it is added. It is worth experimenting, though – check with your bread machine instructions manual to see how much the manufacturer recommends.

Fibre

For health reasons we are encouraged to eat more fibre in our diet, and bread is an excellent way to increase our intake. If you find 100% wholemeal flour too heavy-going, use white flour and add an extra form of fibre. Extra liquid is usually added to a higher-fibre bread dough as the increased fibre absorbs more liquid:

Wheat bran and oat bran – add a maximum of 1 Tbsp per 125g (4oz) flour to prevent the gluten activity from being restricted.

Wheatgerm – add in the quantities stated above; this also adds a nutty flavour and is an excellent source of vitamin E.

Rolled oats – adds a chewy texture and slight nuttiness to a loaf, and can be used in small amounts in conjunction with bread flour.

Unsweetened muesli – a ready-made combination of rolled oats, wheat flakes, chopped nuts and dried fruit that will add flavour, texture and nutritional value to a bread dough.
Cooked brown and wild rice – can be added to a bread dough mixture and will help give a moist crumb, slightly chewy texture and nutty flavour.

Ascorbic acid

You may find some recipes that still encourage the addition of a vitamin C tablet or powder to a wholemeal bread dough to improve the rise and texture of the finished loaf. It is worth experimenting to see if you like the texture. Check with your bread machine instructions manual to see how much the manufacturer recommends you add. Lemon juice is sometimes added to a mixture to help with the rise and give a lighter texture. If you want to experiment, try adding 1 tsp lemon juice per 250g (8oz) wholemeal bread flour.

Commercial dough conditioners

You can buy commercially produced conditioners as an aid to improving the rise and texture of your finished loaf. These are usually added to breads that are produced commercially to help stabilise the gluten and retain as much air as possible during the cooking process. A dough relaxer will help to soften the gluten and gives a softer, more moist result with improved keeping qualities. A dough enhancer adds extra gluten to give a lighter, softly chewy texture.

Xanthan gum

Also known as corn-sugar gum and given the food additive reference number E415. It is a by-product that occurs naturally when carbohydrates are fermented by bacteria. The gum is fibrous but dissolves in water to form a sticky gel and it is this property that gives it use as a stabiliser and emulsifier particularly with gluten-free flours, where elasticity cannot be developed. It is available from health food shops and stockists of special dietary products, and is often already added to gluten-free baking products. Refer to the manufacturer's packaging label for advice on usage quantities.

Flavourings

Seasonings such as dried and freshly chopped herbs, chillies, ground and crushed whole spices, finely grated citrus rind and essences can really transform the humble loaf. Lightly toasting whole spices by dry-roasting them in a hot frying pan for a few minutes will add depth and earthiness to their natural flavour.

Small dried fruits and chopped larger ones, nuts, seeds, and preserved chopped ginger and mixed citrus peel should be added in accordance with your bread machine instructions manual, as should small pieces of cooked meats such as ham, bacon, chorizo and salami. Some machines have a beeping mechanism prior to the second kneading which indicates when you can add such ingredients, and more sophisticated machines may have a dispenser for adding flavourings at a given point during the cycle. I add all my extras at the beginning of the process as I have found that the kneading blade is not sharp enough to blend things up entirely.

Chocolate can be melted into the liquid at the start of the programme, or cocoa can be mixed with the flour; small chocolate pieces such as polka dots will stay fairly whole during the kneading and cooking process for extra chocolate flavour and molten texture.

Grated raw and cooked vegetables, soaked and finely chopped dried vegetables – use the soaking liquid for extra flavour – mashed cooked vegetables, tinned sweetcorn, chopped stoned olives, mashed banana, small berries, chopped apple and stewed fruit can all be used, but the texture is often heavier and the loaf rise will not be as good because of the increased bulk and extra water content. You can certainly make some interesting colours, flavours and textures by experimenting with these types of ingredients.

NOTE: One of our most popular seasonings is garlic. Fresh garlic has natural anti-fungal properties however, so will inhibit the function of yeast.

I suggest you use fresh garlic sparingly, slightly increasing the yeast quantity if necessary, or that you use dried garlic powder or replace the salt with garlic-flavoured salt.

BREAD MACHINE BASICS

The main justification for investing in a bread machine is the same as for the majority of other kitchen gadgets: it's labour-saving. Although machines vary in price, shape, size and colour, they all work on the same basic principles and do roughly the same things, e.g. make a white loaf, wholemeal loaf and bread dough, and have a rapid setting. The machines at the lower end of the price scale will offer fewer programmes on top of the basics compared with machines that cost twice or three times as much, so personal preference comes into play when you do your research.

A bread machine mixes, kneads, proves and bakes a loaf in accordance with the ingredients and the quantities used. You have to measure the ingredients out, put them in the bread pan, close the lid then select a programme and press start. All machines have a removable non-stick bread pan with a handle and a kneading blade or paddle. Once the blade is fitted into the machine, it turns round to mix and knead the ingredients. The snug-fitting lid ensures that the dough is kept at the right temperature during proving and baking. There is an air vent to prevent over-heating and some machines have a viewing window so you can see what's going on.

The control panel is on the top or side and contains the programme menu and the time display. This acts as a status indicator to show you how much time is left and what stage your loaf has reached. You can also programme a delayed start using the timer to enable you to have freshly baked bread at a specific time — you can do this the night before so that you have fresh bread ready for breakfast (the maximum delay is about 12 hours).

Most machines have a power failure mechanism which kicks in if the machine gets accidentally switched off during a programme; once the power supply is resumed the programme continues as before. This is usually limited to 10–30 minutes without power. Depending on the stage the dough has reached when the power failure occurred, it may remain unaffected.

The size and shape of the loaf is determined by the shape of the bread pan. Larger machines tend to have an oblong pan which gives a more traditional "farmhouse" loaf, while compact models have a tall, square pan. Loaves cooked in these machines can be turned on their sides when ready for slicing, to make smaller neat squared-off slices. The size of the loaf can be varied by the quantities of ingredients used. Loaf sizes can vary from 500g (1lb) through to 1.5kg (3lb). Usually a machine will make at least a 750-g (1½-lb) and a 1-kg (2-lb) loaf, and all my recipes in the book are geared towards the 1-kg (2-lb) loaf — you will probably have to select the size of loaf you are making on the control panel. If your machine grades the size of loaf as small, medium or large, take a look through the manufacturer's instructions manual and select the size suitable for a recipe using about 500g (1lb) flour. You can also set the crust colour to suit your personal preference (I usually use the medium setting) and this will be something with which you can experiment as you get more experienced. As a general rule, loaves with extra sugar or added protein-rich foods such as eggs will brown more than plainer loaves, so you may want to select a lighter crust setting when cooking these types of bread.

Many machines have a preheating cycle built

in to all the conventional programmes, and this means you can use ingredients straight from the fridge. For quicker cycles, however, you will usually be advised to warm the liquid and use ingredients at room temperature – check in your instructions manual. Once the machine has finished a cycle, it will usually keep the loaf warm for up to 1 hour, although it is advisable to take the loaf out of the machine as soon as it is ready for best results. There will be operating lights and beeps that occur at certain times during programmes, and this is to advise you when to add ingredients such as chopped fruit and nuts. Some machines have a dispenser, which drops such additions automatically into the pan at a designated time.

I have not used these features in this book and found that adding all the ingredients at the start provided perfectly acceptable results. The lights and beeps also occur when a programme is starting, has finished, or if an error occurs.

Programmes

This is a general guide to bread machine settings. NOTE: You should always read through the instructions manual that comes with your machine before you start to familiarize yourself with your machine's particular quirks. The time each programme takes to perform a complete cycle will vary from machine to machine, and your machine will indicate the length of time involved at the start of the programme.

Basic or normal – for producing loaves using white bread or soft-grain white bread flour as a major ingredient, in approx. 3–4 hours.

Whole wheat – for loaves made with wholemeal bread flour, or breads with cereal and grains like rye or Granary® in about 3½– 5 hours.

Rapid or quick – can produce a white or wholemeal loaf between 2 and 3 hours. The rising time is shorter so the texture may be denser than that of a loaf cooked on a longer cycle. I use this cycle for low-gluten or gluten-free mixes which don't require the extra time for gluten development.

French – for loaves needing a crisp crust and open texture, and those with little or no fat and/or sugar included. This programme has a longer rising cycle and often cooks at a higher temperature.

Sweet – often not included if a machine has a crust colour control. Designed for breads with a high fat and/or sugar content, which have a tendency to over-brown on a normal setting. Cake or dessert – a programme designed for use only in conjunction with your manufacturer's instructions manual and recipes. This programme mixes and then bakes non-yeasted mixtures in accordance with quantities to suit the machine. For this reason, there are no recipes in this book using this setting.

Bake only – this enables you to bake cakes and tea loaves that you have premixed. You simply line the bread pan and set the timer to cook. Timers usually have a maximum limit of around 1½ hours. It is not suitable for bakes that need to go into a hot oven, i.e. sponge cakes. NOTE: Refer to the manufacturer's guidelines when using this setting. In some machines the element is closer to the pan than in others and therefore these machines cook more quickly. As a general guideline, if the manufacturer suggests baking using small amounts of sugar, then reduce each of my cooking times by 10–15 minutes in order to prevent over-browning. This facility also enables you to extend the standard baking time on other programmes if you prefer a particularly dark crust.

Dough – this cycle mixes, kneads and proves dough, allowing you to shape rolls, pastries etc. and then bake them in a conventional oven. Some machines also have a dough cycle for different types of dough, e.g. pizza and focaccia. All recipes in the Dough chapter of this book (see pages 100–133) were tested on a basic dough setting. See notes on shaping dough (page 23).

Other programmes and features:

Super rapid – allows you to make and cook a basic white loaf in under 1 hour. The recipe will require more yeast than the quantity used in other loaves.

Jam – add fruit and sugar and set to the jam programme. When the cycle is complete spoon the jam into sterilized jars and seal as for conventionally cooked jam.

Gluten-free – a setting used in conjunction with the manufacturer's instructions manual and recipe book, often designed for specific gluten-free ready-prepared mixes.

Pasta – for making perfect pasta dough ready for shaping.

Rice – gently steams the rice until it is cooked.

Butter – churns cream into fresh butter in 30 minutes.

BREAD MACHINE GOLDEN RULES

Read the instructions manual before you start – this will explain how your machine works and the step-by-step instructions to follow. It has been specially designed to accompany your machine and that make only. NOTE: You must follow the basic instructions given in the manual if they differ from my instructions or those of any other book you may use.

Measure accurately – I use my own kitchen measuring spoons, a detailed measuring jug and digital scales, and I always use the same ones for all my bread making. I would recommend that you do the same. Measures are level unless stated otherwise. This is important, particularly with ingredients such as yeast. Follow either metric or imperial measures but do not combine the two, as there are slight differences in conversion quantities. NOTE: When it comes to following the recipes in the manufacturer's instructions manual, you should use the plastic spoons and measuring container that come with the machine.

Add the ingredients in sequence – most machines state that the liquid is the first thing that goes into the bread pan, but one of my machines calls for the yeast to go in first – in this instance you would have to turn the list of ingredients in this book round the other way and start with the last on the list. NOTE: Always follow the order stated in your instructions manual – don't deviate from this.

Keep the yeast away from the liquid – unlike other types of yeast, the fast-acting yeast used in bread-machine baking does not need pre-activating. Fast-acting yeast should only be mixed with dry ingredients. Care should also be taken to separate the yeast from the salt and sugar – avoid piling the yeast on top of or underneath the salt and/or sugar, as this can inhibit its activation. Adding the flour in two stages helps to alleviate this potential problem.

Position your machine correctly – make sure the bread machine is on a stable work surface, away from direct sunlight, draughts or heat sources, and do not move the machine while it is working. Make sure there is plenty of space around the machine so that it doesn't over-heat; it may get quite hot during the baking cycle.

Do not peek! – apart from when the machine beeps to let you know you can add chopped fruit etc. you should not lift the lid, especially during the proving or baking cycles, as the controlled atmosphere within the machine will be disturbed and affect the finished loaf. If you are naturally curious, a machine with a viewing window is vital!

Remove the kneading blade or paddle from a loaf safely – from time to time, when you come to turn your freshly baked loaf out of the pan, you will find that the kneading blade has become embedded in the bottom of the loaf. It will of course be very hot and the loaf will be quite soft. Allow the loaf to cool for about 1 hour and then prise the blade from the loaf using a utensil that won't scratch the non-stick blade, such as a rigid plastic spatula.

Keep your machine and bread pan clean – you

should clean the bread pan and blade after each use with mild detergent only. Always unplug and cool the machine before cleaning. If the blade gets stuck in the pan pour warm water into the pan and soak for up to 10 minutes to remove. Rinse the inside of the pan with mild detergent, but do not submerge in water. The outside of the machine can be easily wiped down with a clean damp cloth and mild detergent. If something has baked on, use a non-scratch scourer to remove it. Exceptional care must be taken when cleaning the inside of the machine to avoid damaging the temperature sensor – refer to the manufacturer's instructions manual for specific instructions. The parts of your machine are unlikely to be dishwasher-safe.

Be prepared to have a few disasters until you get to know your machine, as all machines vary – I have included a Troubleshooting guide (see pages 26–27) to help you work out what might have gone wrong.

HANDY HINTS

Shaping

If you want to experiment with bread dough and make different shaped rolls to impress your guests, here are some ideas to help you. Using 1 quantity of Simple white loaf (see page 32), Simple wholemeal loaf (see page 35) or Malted grain loaf (see page 41) ingredients set on the dough setting, you will be able to make 12 rolls.

When the dough cycle is complete, turn the dough on to a lightly floured surface and knead into a smooth, round ball. Divide into 12 equal pieces and shape as desired:

Dinner rolls

Roll the pieces into small rounds and place on a large greased baking sheet. Using kitchen scissors, cut a cross in the top of each and pull back the points.

Splits

Roll the pieces into small balls and then into ovals. Place on a large greased baking sheet. Using a sharp knife, press down the centre of each roll, lengthways, taking care not to cut all the way through.

Knots

Roll the pieces into small balls and then into a sausage shape about 15cm (6 in) long. Tie into a simple, loose knot and place on a large greased baking sheet.

Parker House

Roll the dough pieces into small balls and then press into small neat circles about 1cm (1/2in) thick. Brush with a little glaze and fold over, ensuring the top piece of dough overlaps the bottom. Press down lightly on the folded edge. Transfer to a large greased baking sheet.

Cooking

Cover the rolls with oiled clingfilm and set aside in a warm place for about 30 minutes until risen. Take care not to over-prove or the rolls will lose their shape during cooking. Preheat the oven to 220°C/425°F/Gas mark 7, glaze and finish as desired (see pages 27–28) and bake for 10–15 minutes until golden and risen. Transfer to a wire rack to cool. Best served warm.

Glazes and finishes

Flour

Lightly dusting a proved loaf with flour before conventional baking will ensure a soft crust.

Beaten egg glaze

Whisk together 1 egg and 1 Tbsp water with a pinch of salt until well beaten. If you brush a loaf with this mixture as soon as it comes out of the bread machine, the egg will cook in the heat and you will have a smooth, shiny finish. Alternatively, brush on before conventional baking.

Egg white glaze

Whisk together 1 egg white and 1 Tbsp water with a pinch of salt until well beaten. If you brush a loaf with this mixture as soon as it comes out of the bread machine, the egg white will cook in the heat and you will have a clear, glossy finish. Alternatively, brush on before conventional baking.

Egg yolk glaze

Whisk together 1 egg yolk and 1 Tbsp milk with a pinch of salt until well beaten. If you brush a loaf with this mixture as soon as it comes out of the bread machine, the egg yolk will cook in the heat and you will have a rich, golden finish. Alternatively, brush on before conventional baking.

Water

Brushing water on to a proved loaf, or spraying with a light mister spray just before conventional baking will give a crisp, golden crust. Used for French bread.

Jam, honey and maple syrup glaze

Sieve 2 Tbsp jam of your choice (apricot is the best choice) and mix with 1–2 tsp warm water. Brush over baked bread, buns and pastries as soon as they come out of the bread machine to give a sweet and sticky finish. Warmed clear honey and maple syrup can be used in the same way. Alternatively, brush on before conventional baking.

Melted butter and olive oil

Brush over warm bread after it has baked to soften the crust and add richness.

Glacé icing

Sift 115g (4oz) icing sugar into a bowl and gradually add about 1 Tbsp warm water, mixing to form a thickish icing. Add a few drops of vanilla, coffee or almond essence if you require a little flavouring, and add a little more water if you want to drizzle the icing more easily.

Other toppings

To add texture and variety, sprinkle a glazed loaf with small seeds, finely chopped or flaked nuts, rolled oats, white bran, grated cheese, softly cooked sliced onion, coarse salt, polenta, ground black pepper or a light dusting of chilli powder or paprika. Sweet loaves can be dusted with coarse sugar such as demerara or crushed sugar lumps, and finished loaves can be dusted with icing sugar.

Storing dough and bread

Freshly baked bread is best eaten within 2–3 days. Once the bread has cooled, wrap it in foil or a food-safe plastic bag, and seal it well. A crisp crust will soften once wrapped, so until you cut into the loaf, it is best left unwrapped. Bread starts to go stale quite quickly once it is cut, so wrap well to preserve it as much as possible. Storing bread in the fridge will dry it out.

For longer storage, freezing is the best option. Either slice beforehand for convenience or leave whole, and place in a large freezer bag. Seal and freeze for up to 3 months. Thaw bread in the freezer bag at room temperature. Rolls and smaller breads such as pittas, naans and baguettes are best eaten on the day they are made, but they freeze well – seal well in a freezer bag and freeze for up to 3 months.

Prepared dough can be kept in the fridge in an oiled bowl, covered with clingfilm, for about 2 days. Check the dough and knock it back occasionally if it starts to rise too much. Bring back to room temperature before shaping, proving and baking in accordance with your recipe. Rolls can be prepared and shaped the night before, ready for baking the next day – cover with oiled clingfilm and store in the fridge on baking sheets. Bring back to room temperature before proving and baking. You can freeze bread dough in a freezer bag for up to 1 month. Thaw overnight in the fridge and bring back to room temperature before using.

Adapting recipes and using bread mixes

If you've got some favourite recipes you would like to try in your bread machine, here are a few pointers to take into consideration before you begin:

• Make sure your bread pan can take the quantity of ingredients in your recipe. Each model will have a maximum capacity, so check in the manufacturer's instructions manual.

• Find a similar recipe in your instructions manual or a bread machine recipe book to give you an idea of the quantities to use and which programme to choose. The flour versus liquid ratio is the most crucial to get right for success.

• Be prepared to make adjustments to your recipe – cooking in a bread machine is very different to conventional baking. You may have to make sacrifices, such as only making the dough in your machine, then shaping, proving and baking conventionally.

• Keep a close check on a recipe you're cooking for the first time and make notes so that you know what to do (or change) the next time.

• Refer to your instructions manual when using ready-prepared bread mixes as some have specific instructions. If the manual doesn't have instructions, then follow the guidelines on the packet. Above all, make sure your machine can cope with the volume of ingredients being used.

TROUBLESHOOTING

Even the most experienced cook will have a few teething problems when using a bread machine for the first time. Don't be put off, just try and be as careful as you can and don't rush the preparation. I have compiled a list of the most common problems and how to rectify them, and your instructions manual will have a whole host of others specifically for your model.

Bread rises:

• too much – too much yeast and/or water or sugar added. Not enough salt. Measure accurately, and reduce or increase quantities slightly if appropriate.

• too little – insufficient yeast was added or the yeast wasn't fresh. The yeast has come into contact with the liquid, salt or sugar before the cycle starts. Too little sugar was added, or too much salt. Measure accurately, and reduce or increase quantities slightly if appropriate. Use only the freshest ingredients, and use them in the correct sequence.

Bread texture is:

• very dense, heavy and moist – too much liquid added or extra liquid added with additional ingredients such as fruit or vegetables. Measure accurately, and reduce liquid quantity slightly, if appropriate.

• crumbly, dry and coarse – too little liquid added or extra bulk has been added to the ingredients such as added grains, bran or other cereals. Measure accurately, and increase liquid quantity

slightly, if appropriate. Reduce quantities of additional ingredients. Note that breads low in fat dry out more quickly, and bread left too long to cool before storage can become dried out.

• holey – the dough is too wet, so try using less liquid. No, or insufficient, salt was added – measure accurately. External conditions such as warm weather or high humidity, which can make the yeast work too quickly, can also affect the performance of your bread machine. Try using your machine when the weather gets cooler.

The bread crust is:

• burnt – too much sugar for normal setting. Try a lighter crust setting or select the sweet programme if you have one.

• pale – replace water with protein-rich ingredients such as dried or fresh milk. Set the crust to a darker setting. Add a little more sugar.

• shrivelled or puckered – this occurs if the loaf has been left in the machine too long after baking. Remove from the machine as soon as possible, and allow to cool on a wire rack.

Overall appearance of the loaf is:

• lopsided – too little liquid (if the dough is too stiff, it can't rise properly). Add 2 tsp more if necessary.

• sunk in the middle – too much liquid or yeast was added – measure accurately. If no salt was added, the bread will rise and collapse as the yeast has over-worked. If you open the lid during proving or baking, the loaf will also be likely to sink.

Ingredients not mixed properly:

Check if the kneading blade was inserted properly. Too much flour was added – measure accurately. Insufficient liquid will mean that there isn't enough to bind the ingredients together. An interruption in power can also result in a poor finished result. If you have added chopped fruit or nuts and they have not mixed properly, make sure you add them at the beginning or when the machine instructs you to make any additions.

When using the dough setting the dough is:

• dry and crumbly – insufficient liquid has been added. Add more water, 1 Tbsp at a time, during the kneading cycle to achieve correct consistency.

• sticky and too soft – too much liquid has been added. Add more flour, 1 Tbsp at a time, during kneading cycle to achieve correct consistency.

Loaves

30

Nothing beats the homely and comforting smell of freshly baked bread, and using your bread machine means you can have fresh bread with the minimum of effort whenever you want. In this chapter there are recipes to get you familiarized with your machine, from the simple basics to the more flavoursome loaves with added ingredients. All of these loaves are mixed, kneaded, proved and baked in the machine – all you have to do is weigh out the ingredients then sit back and wait for the finished result!

After you have worked your way through some of the plainer, standard loaves, you'll see how easy bread making can be and will be inspired to try some of your own combinations. I suggest you start with the Simple white loaf (see page 32) and Simple wholemeal loaf (see page 35).
I have also included recipes that use a sourdough starter instead of yeast – a very natural method of helping bread to rise. This requires a little advance preparation but, once you have developed the starter, you can keep replenishing it and you'll be able to make all your bread in this way if you want to.

Simple white loaf

Simplicity {Makes 1 large loaf } Approx 800g/1lb 10oz

250ml (8fl oz) water

2 Tbsp sunflower oil

2 Tbsp caster sugar

2 tsp salt

500g (1lb) strong plain
white flour

2 tsp instant or fast-acting
dried yeast

Egg yolk glaze (see page 25)

2 Tbsp sesame or poppy seeds
(optional)

Pour the water into the bread pan first unless otherwise directed – some machines call for the yeast to be added first. Add the oil and half the flour. Sprinkle over the salt, sugar and remaining flour, reserving 1 Tbsp. Make a small indentation in the top and pile the yeast in the centre.

   Fit the pan into the bread machine and set to the basic/normal setting, medium crust, 1-kg (2-lb) loaf size. Press Start.

   When the bread is ready, carefully shake the loaf to remove it from the pan and transfer to a wire rack, standing the loaf the correct way up. Dust lightly with the remaining flour and allow to cool for at least 1 hour before removing the kneading blade if necessary.

An excellent recipe to get you started. It's straightforward and gives a perfect result so you'll be inspired to carry on experimenting. The crust is floured and lightly golden and the bread inside is soft and light.

For a richer, more golden appearance, add 2 Tbsp skimmed milk powder or granules with the second quantity of flour.

Simple wholemeal loaf

Wholesome {Makes 1 large loaf } Approx 850g/1lb 12oz

350ml (12fl oz) water

30g (1oz) unsalted butter

500g (1lb) + 1 Tbsp strong
wholemeal bread flour

1½ tsp salt

1½ Tbsp light brown sugar

1 tsp instant or fast-acting
dried yeast

Pour the water into the bread pan first unless otherwise directed – some machines call for the yeast to be added first. Add the butter and half the flour. Sprinkle over the salt, sugar and remaining flour, reserving 1 Tbsp. Make a small indentation in the top and pile the yeast in the centre.

Fit the pan into the bread machine and set to the whole wheat setting, medium crust, 1-kg (2-lb) loaf size. Press Start.

When the bread is ready, carefully shake the loaf to remove it from the pan and transfer to a wire rack, standing the loaf the correct way up. Dust lightly with remaining flour and allow to cool for at least 1 hour before removing the kneading blade if necessary.

A much denser-textured loaf, which can be lightened if preferred by using half wholemeal and half strong white bread flour. You'll find the flavour hearty and rustic, suitable for eating any time.

The increased fibre content of wholemeal flour makes it nutritious, but you do need to increase the amount of water as wholemeal flour is more absorbent. Traditionally, vitamin C (ascorbic acid) was added to wholemeal bread mixes to improve the rise and volume of the loaf. Nowadays, the instant or fast-acting dried yeast includes vitamin C; however, you might like to experiment by adding ¼ tsp vitamin C powder to your mixture and see if you prefer the resulting loaf. Add it with the second quantity of flour.

Soft-grain bread

Al dente {Makes 1 large loaf} Approx 800g/1lb 10oz

300ml (10fl oz) water

2 Tbsp sunflower oil

500g (1lb) soft-grain strong white bread flour

1½ tsp salt

1 Tbsp runny honey

1 tsp instant or fast-acting dried yeast

Pour the water into the bread pan first unless otherwise directed – some machines call for the yeast to be added first. Add the oil and half the flour. Sprinkle over the salt, honey and remaining flour. Make a small indentation in the top and pile the yeast in the centre.

Fit the pan into the bread machine and set to the basic/normal setting, medium crust, 1-kg (2-lb) loaf size. Press Start.

When the bread is ready, carefully shake the loaf to remove it from the pan and transfer to a wire rack, standing the loaf the correct way up. Allow to cool for at least 1 hour before removing the kneading blade if necessary.

This makes a delicious sandwich loaf. Based on a traditional white loaf recipe, it is made with white bread flour and kibbled or cracked grains of rye and wheat. This gives it a more "chewy" texture and the added fibre gives more flavour.

Malted grain loaf

Malty sweet {Makes 1 large loaf} Approx 800g/1lb 10oz

350ml (12fl oz) water

30g (1oz) unsalted butter

500g (1lb) Granary® malted brown bread flour or country grain

1½ tsp salt

1 Tbsp malt extract

1 tsp instant or fast-acting dried yeast

Pour the water into the bread pan first unless otherwise directed – some machines call for the yeast to be added first. Add the butter and half the flour. Sprinkle over the salt, and add the malt extract and remaining flour. Make a small indentation in the top and pile the yeast in the centre.

Fit the pan into the bread machine and set to the whole wheat setting, medium crust, 1-kg (2-lb) loaf size. Press Start.

When the bread is ready, carefully shake the loaf to remove it from the pan and transfer to a wire rack, standing the loaf the correct way up. Allow to cool for at least 1 hour before removing the kneading blade if necessary.

Several flour blends will give you a similar result for this loaf. Granary® flour, malthouse flour or a country grain flour are some you might come across. The bread has a slight sweetness and the grains in the flour give it a little crunchiness; it goes well with both sweet and savoury accompaniments.

Seeded loaf

Crunchy {Makes 1 large loaf} Approx 800g/1lb 10oz

350ml (12fl oz) water

2 Tbsp sunflower oil

250g (8oz) strong white bread flour

250g (8oz) strong wholemeal
bread flour

1½ tsp salt

1½ Tbsp light brown sugar

1 Tbsp + 2 tsp poppy seeds

1 tsp toasted sesame seeds

2 tsp flax seeds (linseeds)

15g (½oz) pumpkin seeds,
lightly crushed

15g (½oz) toasted sunflower seeds, lightly
crushed

2 tsp instant or fast-acting
dried yeast

Beaten egg glaze (see page 24)

Pour the water into the bread pan first unless otherwise directed – some machines call for the yeast to be added first. Add the oil and half of both flours. Sprinkle over the salt, sugar, all the seeds except for 2 tsp poppy seeds, and then the remaining flour. Make a small indentation in the top and pile the yeast in the centre.

Fit the pan into the bread machine and set to the whole wheat setting, medium crust, 1-kg (2-lb) loaf size. Press Start.

When the bread is ready, carefully shake the loaf to remove it from the pan and transfer to a wire rack, standing the loaf the correct way up. Immediately brush with egg glaze and sprinkle with the remaining poppy seeds. Allow to cool for at least 1 hour before removing the kneading blade if necessary.

Once opened, store nuts and seeds in an airtight container in the refrigerator to keep them fresh.

Seeds are full of nutritional goodness and flavour so this loaf is guaranteed to be popular. You need to lightly crush the larger seeds just before adding them to the mixture to give an even texture. One of my favourite sandwich fillings goes well with this bread: hummus, sprouting mung beans and alfalfa seeds with homemade coleslaw. Delicious!

Light rye loaf

Spiced {Makes 1 large loaf } Approx 850g/1lb 12oz

350ml (12fl oz) lukewarm water

2 tsp lemon juice

2 Tbsp sunflower oil

350g (12oz) strong white bread flour

150g (5oz) rye flour

1½ tsp salt

1½ Tbsp light brown sugar

1 Tbsp cumin seeds, toasted and lightly crushed

1 tsp instant or fast-acting dried yeast

Pour the water into the bread pan first unless otherwise directed – some machines call for the yeast to be added first. Add the lemon juice, oil and half of both flours. Sprinkle over the salt, sugar, seeds and then the remaining flour. Make a small indentation in the top and pile the yeast in the centre.

Fit the pan into the bread machine and set to the basic/normal setting, medium crust, 1-kg (2-lb) loaf size. Press Start.

When the bread is ready, carefully shake the loaf to remove it from the pan and transfer to a wire rack, standing the loaf the correct way up. Allow to cool for at least 1 hour before removing the kneading blade if necessary.

This loaf is rich in flavour, with a lighter texture than an all-wholemeal loaf. Cumin seeds are used as a flavouring, making it excellent served with thickly sliced ham and sweet mango chutney.

To toast seeds – place in a heavy-based pan and cook, stirring, over a medium heat for 4–5 minutes until lightly toasted and fragrant. Transfer to a heatproof plate and set aside to cool.

Darker rye loaf

Fragrant {Makes 1 large loaf } Approx 900g/2lb

350ml (12fl oz) lukewarm
water

2 tsp lemon juice

1 Tbsp treacle or molasses

2 Tbsp sunflower oil

250g (8oz) strong white bread
flour

250g (8oz) rye flour

1½ tsp salt

2 Tbsp caraway seeds

1½ tsp instant or fast-acting
dried yeast

Pour the water into the bread pan first unless otherwise directed – some machines call for the yeast to be added first. Add the oil and half of both flours. Sprinkle over the salt, sugar, all the seeds except for 2 tsp poppy seeds, and then the remaining flour. Make a small indentation in the top and pile the yeast in the centre.

Fit the pan into the bread machine and set to the whole wheat setting, medium crust, 1-kg (2-lb) loaf size. Press Start.

When the bread is ready, carefully shake the loaf to remove it from the pan and transfer to a wire rack, standing the loaf the correct way up. Immediately brush with egg glaze and sprinkle with the remaining poppy seeds. Allow to cool for at least 1 hour before removing the kneading blade if necessary.

Not as rich as German pumpernickel bread, but packed full of the familiar flavour that enriching a loaf with rye flour, caraway seeds and treacle or molasses provides. The flavour of rye goes particularly well with smoked salmon, dill and pickles. Use a little soft cheese for spreading, instead of butter.

Toasted nutty bread

Naturally sweet {Makes 1 large loaf } Approx 900g/2lb

350ml (12fl oz) unsweetened apple juice, at room temperature

2 Tbsp sunflower oil

400g (14oz) strong wholemeal bread flour

100g (3½oz) buckwheat flour

1½ tsp salt

2 tsp maple syrup

30g (1oz) toasted hazelnuts, lightly crushed

30g (1oz) toasted almonds, lightly crushed

15g (½oz) toasted unsalted cashew nuts, lightly crushed

1 tsp instant or fast-acting dried yeast

Pour the apple juice into the bread pan first unless otherwise directed – some machines call for the yeast to be added first. Add the oil and half of both flours. Sprinkle over the salt, 1 tsp maple syrup, all the nuts and then the remaining flour. Make a small indentation in the top and pile the yeast in the centre.

Fit the pan into the bread machine and set to the whole wheat setting, medium crust, 1-kg (2-lb) loaf size. Press Start.

When the bread is ready, carefully shake the loaf to remove it from the pan and transfer to a wire rack, standing the loaf the correct way up. Brush with the remaining maple syrup and allow to cool for at least 1 hour before removing the kneading blade if necessary.

With very little added sugar, this loaf is sweetened by the ingredients themselves. Toasting nuts before you use them brings out a mellow flavour, which develops further on baking. This loaf tastes good on its own or topped with a simple Nut paste (see page 170).

Buckwheat flour is gluten-free so you'll find the texture of this bread much denser and the rise will not be as good as a more traditional all-wholemeal loaf.

Simple gluten-free loaf

Close-textured {Makes 1 large loaf } Approx 1kg/2lb 2oz

350ml (12fl oz) lukewarm water

2 tsp lemon juice

2 medium eggs, at room temperature

2 Tbsp + 1 tsp sunflower oil

500g (1lb) gluten-free white bread flour

1 tsp salt

2 Tbsp + 1 tsp caster sugar

2 tsp instant or fast-acting dried yeast

Mix the water, lemon juice and eggs together and pour into the bread pan first unless otherwise directed – some machines call for the yeast to be added first. Add the oil and half the flour. Sprinkle over the salt and sugar, and add the remaining flour. Make a small indentation in the top and pile the yeast in the centre.

Fit the pan into the bread machine and set to the rapid or quick setting, medium crust, 1-kg (2-lb) loaf size. Press Start.

When the bread is ready, carefully shake the loaf to remove it from the pan and transfer to a wire rack, standing the loaf the correct way up. Allow to cool for at least 1 hour before removing the kneading blade if necessary.

With intolerance to gluten becoming increasingly common, there is a huge demand for gluten-free products. As well as the naturally gluten-free grains, there are blends and mixes available specifically designed for bread making. This recipe is tailored to suit such a flour and offers a great alternative to traditional wheat breads.

If you are making this loaf for dietary reasons, it is very important to avoid any cross-contamination with flours that contain gluten. In order to reduce the risk, make sure the pan, kneading blade and all utensils have been thoroughly cleaned since the last time you used the machine.

Black bread

Robust {Makes 1 large loaf} Approx 850g/1lb 12oz

350ml (12fl oz) lukewarm water

2 tsp lemon juice

1 Tbsp treacle or molasses

2 Tbsp sunflower oil

250g (8oz) strong wholemeal
bread flour

125g (4½oz) rye flour

125g (4½oz) buckwheat flour

2 Tbsp cocoa powder

1 Tbsp instant coffee granules

1½ tsp salt

1½ tsp instant or fast-acting
dried yeast

Blend the water, lemon juice and treacle together and pour into the bread pan first unless otherwise directed – some machines call for the yeast to be added first. Add the oil and half of the flours. Sprinkle over the cocoa, coffee and salt, and then the remaining flour. Make a small indentation in the top and pile the yeast in the centre.

Fit the pan into the bread machine and set to the rapid bake or quick setting, 1-kg (2-lb) loaf size. Press Start.

When the bread is ready, carefully shake the loaf to remove it from the pan and transfer to a wire rack, standing the loaf the correct way up. Allow to cool for at least 1 hour before removing the kneading blade if necessary.

This is the darkest and richest of my rye loaf recipes and includes coffee and cocoa powder to darken it. The texture is cake-like and close. Slice it thinly and use as a base for open sandwiches topped with liver pâtés and pickles, or pile high with sliced pastrami, watercress and horseradish sauce.

Milk loaf

Creamy smooth {Makes 1 large loaf} Approx 850g/1lb 12oz

350ml (12fl oz) semi-skimmed milk

30g (1oz) unsalted butter

500g (1lb) + 1 Tbsp strong white bread flour

1½ tsp salt

1½ Tbsp skimmed milk powder

1 Tbsp caster sugar

1 tsp instant or fast-acting dried yeast

Pour the milk into the bread pan first unless otherwise directed – some machines call for the yeast to be added first. Add the butter and half the flour. Sprinkle over the salt, milk powder, sugar and remaining flour, reserving 1 Tbsp. Make a small indentation in the top and pile the yeast in the centre.

Fit the pan into the bread machine and set to the basic/normal setting, medium crust (this gives a very golden and crisp crust; set to light crust if preferred), 1-kg (2-lb) loaf size. Press Start.

When the bread is ready, carefully shake the loaf to remove it from the pan and transfer to a wire rack, standing the loaf the correct way up. Dust lightly with the remaining flour and allow to cool for at least 1 hour before removing the kneading blade if necessary.

Conjuring up memories from childhood, this loaf is enriched with milk to give it a fluffy texture. I remember having this bread on holidays in Devon, spread with Devonshire clotted cream and home-made strawberry jam. I prefer a soft, floured crust, but you could brush the loaf with one of the egg glazes described on pages 23–24 for a chewier top.

Spelt flour loaf

Lightly wheaty {Makes 1 large loaf } Approx 850g/1lb 12oz

400ml (14fl oz) lukewarm water

1 tsp heather or other strong-tasting honey

2 Tbsp extra virgin olive oil

500g (1lb) spelt flour

½ tsp coarse sea salt

2 tsp instant or fast-acting dried yeast

Mix the water and honey together and pour into the bread pan first unless otherwise directed – some machines call for the yeast to be added first. Add the oil and half the flour. Sprinkle over the salt and the remaining flour. Make a small indentation in the top and pile the yeast in the centre.

Fit the pan into the bread machine and set to the rapid bake or quick setting, medium crust, 1-kg (2-lb) loaf size. Press Start.

When the bread is ready, carefully shake the loaf to remove it from the pan and transfer to a wire rack, standing the loaf the correct way up. Allow to cool for at least 1 hour before removing the kneading blade if necessary.

This is the recipe I make most frequently in my bread machine. It has become a staple in my diet since I decided to cut down on my intake of wheat gluten. I use spelt flour in all my cooking and it gives a much lighter result than traditional wholemeal flour. Because it is lower in gluten, the texture is more cake-like. Makes 1 large loaf

I love the flavour of heather honey in this loaf, but if you would prefer a milder flavour then replace it with acacia or clover honey.

Simple sourdough loaf

Natural {Makes 1 large loaf } Approx 900g/2lb

The following three recipes use the same Sourdough starter mixture described on page 13. This is a traditional and natural way to leaven bread and offers the chance to really get back to basics. This rich loaf is good toasted and served with both sweet and savoury toppings.

300ml (10fl oz) Sourdough starter (see page 13)

150ml (5fl oz) lukewarm water

2 Tbsp sunflower oil

400g (14oz) + 1 Tbsp very strong white bread flour

100g (3½oz) strong wholemeal bread flour

1½ tsp salt

1 Tbsp light brown sugar

Pour the starter, water and oil into the bread pan. Add all but 1 Tbsp of the white flour and all the wholemeal flour. Sprinkle over the salt and sugar.

Fit the pan into the bread machine and set to the basic/normal setting, medium crust, 1-kg (2-lb) loaf size. Press Start.

When the bread is ready, carefully shake the loaf to remove it from the pan and transfer to a wire rack, standing the loaf the correct way up. Dust with the remaining white flour and allow to cool for at least 1 hour before removing the kneading blade if necessary.

Olive and pesto sourdough loaf

Italian flavours {Makes 1 large loaf} Approx 1kg/2lb 2oz

300ml (10fl oz) Sourdough starter (see page 13)

150ml (5fl oz) lukewarm water

2 Tbsp fresh pesto sauce

400g (14oz) very strong white bread flour

100g (3½oz) strong wholemeal bread flour

1½ tsp salt

1 Tbsp caster sugar

60g (2oz) dry-packed black olives, stoned and finely chopped

1 Tbsp extra virgin olive oil

Pour the starter and water into the bread pan. Add the pesto sauce and flours. Sprinkle over the salt, sugar and olives.

Fit the pan into the bread machine and set to the basic/normal setting, medium crust, 1-kg (2-lb) loaf size. Press Start.

When the bread is ready, carefully shake the loaf to remove it from the pan and transfer to a wire rack, standing the loaf the correct way up. Immediately brush with olive oil and allow to cool for at least 1 hour before removing the kneading blade if necessary.

This bread is excellent thinly sliced, toasted and spread with a green olive tapénade, with some freshly sliced plum tomatoes and fresh basil. It also makes a good accompaniment to a sweet pepper and tomato soup. I prefer to use the treacly black, dry-packed olives in this recipe – they usually come unstoned, but it's well worth the extra effort to remove them.

Sweet onion sourdough loaf

Sweet and savoury {Makes 1 large loaf} Approx 1kg/2lb 2oz

300ml (10fl oz) Sourdough starter (see page 13)

150ml (5fl oz) lukewarm water

1 Tbsp olive oil

400g (14oz) very strong white bread flour

100g (3½oz) strong wholemeal bread flour

60g (2oz) sultanas

4 Tbsp crisp dried chopped onion

1½ tsp salt

1 Tbsp caster sugar

Pour the starter and water into the bread pan. Add the oil and flours. Sprinkle over the sultanas, onion, salt and sugar.

Fit the pan into the bread machine and set to the basic/normal setting, medium crust, 1-kg (2-lb) loaf size. Press Start.

When the bread is ready, carefully shake the loaf to remove it from the pan and transfer to a wire rack, standing the loaf the correct way up. Allow to cool for at least 1 hour before removing the kneading blade if necessary.

Make sure you serve this bread slightly warm so that the flavours really come out. It is the ideal accompaniment to a rich casserole where you need to mop up the juices. It is also good served with mussels cooked in a creamy, garlic-flavoured sauce.

Boston-style brown bread

Homely {Makes 1 large loaf } Approx 1kg/2lb 2oz

300ml (10fl oz) buttermilk

150ml (5fl oz) treacle or molasses

150g (5oz) seedless raisins

200g (7oz) plain flour

150g (5oz) rye flour

150g (5oz) fine cornmeal or polenta

1½ tsp baking powder

1 Tbsp bicarbonate of soda

Pour the buttermilk and treacle into the bread pan. Add the raisins. Sprinkle over the flours and cornmeal or polenta, and then the baking powder and bicarbonate of soda.

Fit the pan into the bread machine and set to the rapid bake or quick setting, 1-kg (2-lb) loaf size. Press Start.

When the bread is ready, carefully shake the loaf to remove it from the pan and transfer to a wire rack, standing the loaf the correct way up. Allow to cool for at least 1 hour before removing the kneading blade if necessary.

Traditionally, this colonial yeast-free bread is steamed in coffee tins and served with spiced baked beans. It has a treacly sweet flavour and can also be served sliced and buttered like a malted fruit loaf. As with all soda breads, it is best eaten on the day it is baked and is best served warm.

New England molasses bread

Treacly {Makes 1 large loaf } Approx 900g/2lb

350ml (12fl oz) water

3 Tbsp molasses

1 tsp lemon juice

30g (1oz) unsalted butter

400g (14oz) strong white bread flour

100g (3½oz) polenta

1½ tsp salt

1½ tsp instant or fast-acting
dried yeast

Mix the water and molasses together and pour into the bread pan first unless otherwise directed – some machines call for the yeast to be added first. Add the lemon juice, butter and half the flour. Sprinkle over the polenta and salt, and then the remaining flour. Make a small indentation in the top and pile the yeast in the centre.

Fit the pan into the bread machine and set to the basic/normal setting, medium crust, 1-kg (2-lb) loaf size. Press Start.

When the bread is ready, carefully shake the loaf to remove it from the pan and transfer to a wire rack, standing the loaf the correct way up. Allow to cool for at least 1 hour before removing the kneading blade if necessary.

I first discovered this recipe when looking through an American cookbook. Based on a traditional bread from New England, this loaf has a soft spongy brown crumb and a slight sweetness from the molasses. It can be used with sweet or savoury toppings and dishes alike; try serving it as an accompaniment to a fish or sweetcorn chowder.

Protein-rich loaf

Energising {Makes 1 large loaf } Approx 800g/1lb 10oz

1 medium whole egg + 1 medium egg yolk

Approx. 200ml (7fl oz) lukewarm semi-skimmed milk

30g (1oz) unsalted butter

400g (14oz) strong white bread flour

100g (3½oz) soya flour

1½ tsp salt

1½ Tbsp skimmed milk powder

1 Tbsp caster sugar

1½ tsp instant or fast-acting dried yeast

Beat the egg, egg yolk and milk together in a measuring jug, and make up to the 300ml (10fl oz) level with extra milk if necessary. Pour into the bread pan first unless otherwise directed – some machines call for the yeast to be added first. Add the butter and half of both flours. Sprinkle over the salt, milk powder, sugar and then the remaining flour. Make a small indentation in the top and pile the yeast in the centre.

Fit the pan into the bread machine and set to the basic/normal setting, medium crust (this gives a very golden and crisp crust; set to light crust if preferred), 1-kg (2-lb) loaf size. Press Start.

When the bread is ready, carefully shake the loaf to remove it from the pan and transfer to a wire rack, standing the loaf the correct way up. Allow to cool for at least 1 hour before removing the kneading blade if necessary.

Soya flour is high in protein and gives a golden colour to this loaf. Adding egg gives a rich flavour and flaky crumb, like a brioche loaf. A great breakfast bread, it is good with both sweet and savoury toppings.

The extra protein content of this loaf gives a darker crust. If preferred you may wish to select a lighter crust setting.

High-fibre loaf

Nutritious {Makes 1 large loaf} Approx 830g/1lb 1 1oz

200ml (7fl oz) lukewarm water

150ml (5fl oz) natural yogurt

2 Tbsp sunflower oil

450g (15oz) strong wholemeal bread flour

1½ tsp salt

1½ Tbsp light brown sugar

45g (1½oz) wheat bran

1 tsp instant or fast-acting dried yeast

Mix the water and yogurt together and pour into the bread pan first unless otherwise directed – some machines call for the yeast to be added first.

Add the oil and half the flour. Sprinkle over the salt, sugar, the remaining flour and the wheat bran. Make a small indentation in the top and pile the yeast in the centre.

Fit the pan into the bread machine and set to the whole wheat setting, medium crust, 1-kg (2-lb) loaf size. Press Start.

When the bread is ready, carefully shake the loaf to remove it from the pan and transfer to a wire rack, standing the loaf the correct way up. Allow to cool for at least 1 hour before removing the kneading blade if necessary.

A soft-textured yogurt bread, enriched with bran for extra dietary fibre. It makes a good breakfast loaf, sliced, toasted and spread with jam or marmalade – a good way to start the day.

Breakfast bread

Sweet spice {Makes 1 large loaf } Approx 850g/1lb 12oz

400ml (14fl oz) lukewarm water

1 tsp heather or other strong-tasting honey

30g (1oz) unsalted butter

500g (1lb) spelt flour

4 Tbsp unsweetened (wheat-free) muesli

1 tsp ground cinnamon

1½ tsp coarse sea salt

2 tsp instant or fast-acting dried yeast

Mix the water and honey together and pour into the bread pan first unless otherwise directed – some machines call for the yeast to be added first.

Add the butter and half the flour. Sprinkle over the muesli, cinnamon, salt and remaining flour. Make a small indentation in the top and pile the yeast in the centre.

Fit the pan into the bread machine and set to the rapid bake or quick setting, medium crust, 1-kg (2-lb) loaf size. Press Start.

When the bread is ready, carefully shake the loaf to remove it from the pan and transfer to a wire rack, standing the loaf the correct way up. Allow to cool for at least 1 hour before removing the kneading blade if necessary.

Another loaf using my favourite flour – spelt flour. I use a wheat-free muesli when I make this recipe in order to reduce the wheat gluten content, but it will work with any unsweetened variety. Serve lightly toasted, spread with butter and extra honey.

Carrot and cumin loaf

Earthy and sweet {Makes 1 large loaf} Approx 900g/2lb

350ml (12fl oz) carrot juice,
at room temperature

1 Tbsp mild runny honey

2 Tbsp sunflower oil

500g (1lb) country grain or Granary®
malted brown bread flour

100g (3½oz) grated carrot

60g (2oz) sultanas

1½ tsp salt

2 tsp cumin seeds, toasted

1 tsp instant or fast-acting
dried yeast

Mix the carrot juice and honey together and pour into the bread pan first unless otherwise directed – some machines call for the yeast to be added first. Add the oil and half the flour. Sprinkle over the grated carrot, sultanas, salt, cumin seeds, and then the remaining flour. Make a small indentation in the top and pile the yeast in the centre.

Fit the pan into the bread machine and set to the whole wheat setting, medium crust, 1-kg (2-lb) loaf size. Press Start.

When the bread is ready, carefully shake the loaf to remove it from the pan and transfer to a wire rack, standing the loaf the correct way up. Allow to cool for at least 1 hour before removing the kneading blade if necessary.

A richly coloured loaf with a strong flavour. The cumin seeds add a Middle Eastern flavour, which makes it good with hummus and a Nut or Toasted seed paste (see pages 170–172).

Oatmeal and blueberry bread

Berry fruits {Makes 1 large loaf } Approx 900g/2lb

200ml (7fl oz) water

150ml (5fl oz) buttermilk

30g (1oz) unsalted butter

450g (15oz) strong wholemeal bread flour

1½ tsp salt

1½ Tbsp light brown sugar

60g (2oz) dried blueberries

45g (1½oz) oat bran

1 tsp instant or fast-acting dried yeast

Mix the water and buttermilk together and pour into the bread pan first unless otherwise directed – some machines call for the yeast to be added first. Add the butter and half the flour. Sprinkle over the salt, sugar, blueberries, the remaining flour and the oat bran. Make a small indentation in the top and pile the yeast in the centre.

Fit the pan into the bread machine and set to the whole wheat setting, medium crust, 1-kg (2-lb) loaf size. Press Start.

When the bread is ready, carefully shake the loaf to remove it from the pan and transfer to a wire rack, standing the loaf the correct way up. Allow to cool for at least 1 hour before removing the kneading blade if necessary.

This loaf is a good breakfast bread, toasted and served topped with sliced banana, fresh blueberries and a drizzle of maple syrup.

Nutty sun-dried tomato loaf

Mediterranean flavours {Makes 1 large loaf } Approx 1kg/2lb 2oz

350ml (12floz) lukewarm water

2 tsp lemon juice

2 medium eggs, beaten

2 Tbsp tomato puree

2 Tbsp + 1 tsp olive oil

500g (1lb) gluten-free white bread flour

90g (3oz) toasted pine nuts

60g (2oz) sun-dried tomatoes in oil, drained and finely chopped

1 tsp salt

2 Tbsp + 1 tsp caster sugar

2 tsp instant or easy-blend dried yeast

Mix the water, lemon juice, eggs and tomato purée together and pour into the bread pan first unless otherwise directed – some machines call for the yeast to be added first. Add the oil, half the flour, pine nuts, sun-dried tomatoes, salt and sugar. Sprinkle over the remaining flour and make a small indentation in the top and pile the yeast in the centre.

Fit the pan into the bread machine and set to the rapid bake or quick setting, medium crust, 1-kg (2-lb) loaf size. Press Start.

When the bread is ready, carefully shake the loaf to remove it from the pan and transfer to a wire rack, standing the loaf the correct way up. Allow to cool for at least 1 hour before removing the kneading blade if necessary. Best served warm.

A gluten-free loaf packed full of flavour, with a spongy texture. I've kept the recipe dairy-free as well, to cater for those on a restricted diet. This makes a good open sandwich with fresh basil, sliced ripe beef tomatoes and mozzarella, lightly dressed with olive oil and balsamic vinegar just before eating.

As with all gluten-free loaves, this bread should be stored in a cool dry place and used within two days. Otherwise, it can be sliced and frozen in convenient portions.

Three-cheese and tomato loaf

Contemporary {Makes 1 large loaf } Approx 1kg/2lb 2oz

350ml (12fl oz) tomato juice, at room temperature

1 Tbsp olive oil

500g (1lb) strong wholemeal bread flour

60g (2oz) dolcelatte cheese, crumbled

30g (1oz) gorgonzola cheese, crumbled

60g (2oz) fresh parmesan cheese, finely grated

60g (2oz) sun-dried tomatoes in oil, drained and finely chopped

1 tsp dried oregano

1 tsp salt

1½ Tbsp caster sugar

1 tsp instant or fast-acting dried yeast

Pour the tomato juice into the bread pan first unless otherwise directed – some machines call for the yeast to be added first. Add the oil and half the flour. Sprinkle over the cheeses, sun-dried tomatoes, oregano, salt, sugar and then the remaining flour. Make a small indentation in the top and pile the yeast in the centre.

Fit the pan into the bread machine and set to the whole wheat setting, medium crust, 1-kg (2-lb) loaf size. Press Start.

When the bread is ready, carefully shake the loaf to remove it from the pan and transfer to a wire rack, standing the loaf the correct way up. Allow to cool for at least 1 hour before removing the kneading blade if necessary.

This bread is probably one of the best-known and much loved modern-day loaves. I have kept to Italian cheeses, but others will work just as well. The loaf makes a good sandwich, filled with Italian salami and sliced tomatoes, and a tasty croûton for soups and salads. It is also delicious served warm with pasta or risotto.

Sweet rosemary bread

Fragrant {Makes 1 large loaf } Approx 900g/2lb

400ml (14fl oz) lukewarm water

1 tsp Greek or other strong-tasting honey

3 Tbsp strongly flavoured olive oil

500g (1lb) spelt flour

60g (2oz) no-soak dried figs, finely chopped

1 Tbsp finely chopped fresh rosemary or 1 tsp dried

½ tsp salt

2 tsp instant or fast-acting dried yeast

Mix the water and honey together and pour into the bread pan first unless otherwise directed – some machines call for the yeast to be added first. Add 2 Tbsp oil and half the flour. Sprinkle over the figs, rosemary, salt and the remaining flour. Make a small indentation in the top and pile the yeast in the centre.

Fit the pan into the bread machine and set to the rapid bake or quick setting, medium crust, 1-kg (2-lb) loaf size. Press Start.

When the bread is ready, carefully shake the loaf to remove it from the pan and transfer to a wire rack, standing the loaf the correct way up. Immediately brush with the remaining oil and allow to cool for at least 1 hour before removing the kneading blade if necessary.

The flavours in this loaf remind me of a holiday I had on the Greek island of Kefalonia with my best friend Juliet. We dined out every lunchtime on salads drenched in heavily flavoured olive oil and seasoned with fresh rosemary, and enjoyed sun-ripened fruit and soft cheeses. Crumbled feta or goat's cheese and fresh figs or peaches are the perfect topping for slices of this bread.

Smoky potato and corn bread

Hearty {Makes 1 large loaf } Approx 850g/1lb 12oz

250ml (9fl oz) whole-milk yogurt, at room temperature

2 large eggs, beaten

30g (1oz) unsalted butter

1 tsp olive oil

250g (8oz) fine cornmeal

45g (1½oz) potato flour

150g (5oz) sweetcorn kernels

1 tsp hot smoked chilli powder

4 tsp baking powder

Spoon the yogurt into the bread pan. Add the remaining ingredients, piling the baking powder on top.

Fit the pan into the bread machine and set to the rapid bake or quick setting, 1-kg (2-lb) loaf size. Press Start.

When the bread is ready, carefully shake the loaf to remove it from the pan and transfer to a wire rack, standing the loaf the correct way up. Allow to cool for at least 1 hour before removing the kneading blade if necessary.

Potato makes a soft, starchy flour that gives a close-textured finish. Here it is used with cornmeal to make a substantial soda-style loaf. Serve warm with salads and soups.

Buckwheat, beetroot and caraway loaf

Dynamic {Makes 1 large loaf } Approx 900g/2lb

350ml (12fl oz) water

30g (1oz) unsalted butter

400g (13oz) strong white bread flour

100g (3½oz) buckwheat flour

1½ tsp salt

100g (3½oz) cooked peeled beetroot in

natural juice, drained and grated

1 Tbsp caster sugar

1 tsp caraway seeds

1 tsp instant or fast-acting

dried yeast

Pour the water into the bread pan first unless otherwise directed – some machines call for the yeast to be added first. Add the butter and half the white flour. Sprinkle over the buckwheat flour, salt, beetroot, sugar, seeds and then the remaining white flour. Make a small indentation in the top and pile the yeast in the centre.

Fit the pan into the bread machine and set to the basic/normal setting, medium crust, 1-kg (2-lb) loaf size. Press Start.

When the bread is ready, carefully shake the loaf to remove it from the pan and transfer to a wire rack, standing the loaf the correct way up. Allow to cool for at least 1 hour before removing the kneading blade if necessary.

The crust colour of this bread is like no other – vibrant pink! – and it's guaranteed to be a talking point at the tea or dinner table. I've used buckwheat as it gives an interesting earthy flavour and a spongy, pinkish crumb. Serve this bread with vegetable soups or sweetly spiced dishes such as goulash.

Curried parsnip loaf

Warming {Makes 1 large loaf } Approx 900g/2lb

300ml (10fl oz) water

1 Tbsp sunflower oil

1 Tbsp mild curry paste

400g (14oz) strong white bread flour

100g (3½oz) gram flour

100g (3½oz) cold mashed parsnips

1 tsp black onion seeds

1½ tsp salt

1 Tbsp light brown sugar

1 tsp instant or fast-acting dried yeast

Pour the water into the bread pan first unless otherwise directed – some machines call for the yeast to be added first. Add the oil, curry paste and half the white flour. Add the gram flour and mashed parsnips, and sprinkle over the onion seeds, salt, sugar and remaining white flour. Make a small indentation in the top and pile the yeast in the centre.

Fit the pan into the bread machine and set to the basic/normal setting, medium crust, 1-kg (2-lb) loaf size. Press Start.

When the bread is ready, carefully shake the loaf to remove it from the pan and transfer to a wire rack, standing the loaf the correct way up. Allow to cool for at least 1 hour before removing the kneading blade if necessary.

Parsnips are naturally sweet and their flavour really develops in this bread. Using a mild curry powder adds an extra dimension, and the gram flour (also known as chickpea or besan flour) gives a beany flavour. I think this bread is best served warm, and it goes well with vegetable or lentil soups.

Polenta bread with cheese and crispy bacon

Golden {Makes 1 large loaf } Approx 1kg/2lb 2oz

350ml (12fl oz) semi-skimmed milk

30g (1oz) unsalted butter

400g (14oz) strong white bread flour

100g (3½oz) fine cornmeal or polenta

60g (2oz) cooked crispy smoked bacon, finely chopped

90g (3oz) finely grated fresh parmesan cheese

1½ tsp salt

1 Tbsp caster sugar

1 tsp instant or fast-acting dried yeast

Pour the milk into the bread pan first unless otherwise directed – some machines call for the yeast to be added first. Add the butter and sprinkle over half the flour, cornmeal, bacon, cheese, salt and sugar. Sprinkle over the remaining flour and make a small indentation in the top and pile the yeast in the centre.

Fit the pan into the bread machine and set to the basic/normal setting, medium crust (see tip below), 1-kg (2-lb) loaf size. Press Start.

When the bread is ready, carefully shake the loaf to remove it from the pan and transfer to a wire rack, standing the loaf the correct way up. Allow to cool for at least 1 hour before removing the kneading blade if necessary.

Cornmeal is naturally gluten-free and is commonly used in soda-style breads. This bread is moist and golden yellow in colour, with a rich cheesy flavour. It is best served warm on the day it is made, and is ideal for mopping up a hearty soup or pasta dish.

Porcini and salami bread

Mushroomy {Makes 1 large loaf} Approx 850g/1lb 12oz

60g (2oz) dried porcini mushrooms

300ml (10fl oz) water

3 Tbsp olive oil

500g (1lb) strong white bread flour

60g (2oz) Italian salami, chopped

1 tsp dried oregano

1½ tsp salt

1 Tbsp caster sugar

1 tsp instant or fast-acting

dried yeast

Place the dried mushrooms in a heatproof bowl. Bring the water to the boil and pour over the mushrooms. Set aside to cool.

Drain the mushrooms, reserving the soaking liquid, and chop finely. Make the reserved soaking liquid up to 300ml (10floz) with sufficient cold water and pour into the bread pan first unless otherwise directed – some machines call for the yeast to be added first. Add 2 Tbsp oil and half the flour. Sprinkle over the chopped mushrooms, salami, oregano, salt, sugar and remaining flour. Make a small indentation in the top and pile the yeast in the centre.

Fit the pan into the bread machine and set to the basic/normal setting, medium crust, 1-kg (2-lb) loaf size. Press Start.

When the bread is ready, carefully shake the loaf to remove it from the pan and transfer to a wire rack, standing the loaf the correct way up. Immediately brush with the remaining oil and allow to cool for at least 1 hour before removing the kneading blade if necessary.

If you like the earthy, yeasty flavour of mushrooms, then you'll love this bread. The salami can be left out if you prefer a vegetarian loaf. Serve warm with pasta or risotto.

Sweet potato and chilli bread

Thai flavours {Makes 1 large loaf} Approx 850g/1lb 12oz

300ml (10fl oz) + 2 Tbsp coconut milk

500g (1lb) strong white bread flour

100g (3½oz) cold mashed sweet potato

1½ tsp dried chilli flakes

6 Tbsp finely chopped coriander

1½ tsp salt

1 Tbsp light brown sugar

1 tsp instant or fast-acting dried yeast

½ tsp coriander seeds, toasted and crushed

Pour all but 2 Tbsp coconut milk into the bread pan first unless otherwise directed – some machines call for the yeast to be added first. Add half the flour. Add the sweet potato and sprinkle over 1 tsp chilli flakes, coriander, salt, sugar and the remaining flour. Make a small indentation in the top and pile the yeast in the centre.

Fit the pan into the bread machine and set to the basic/normal setting, medium crust, 1-kg (2-lb) loaf size. Press Start.

When the bread is ready, carefully shake the loaf to remove it from the pan and transfer to a wire rack, standing the loaf the correct way up. Immediately brush with the reserved coconut milk, and sprinkle with the remaining chilli flakes and crushed coriander seeds. Allow to cool for at least 1 hour before removing the kneading blade if necessary.

Thai food has become very popular just about everywhere, and there's no mistaking the distinct combination of flavours. I like this bread simply spread with peanut butter, but it would make an unusual accompaniment to a green or red curry instead of the more usual rice dishes.

Wild rice and cranberry loaf

Sweet and savoury {Makes 1 large loaf } Approx 900g/2lb

250ml (8fl oz) cranberry juice,
at room temperature

30g (1oz) unsalted butter

400g (14oz) strong white bread flour

100g (3½oz) rice flour

100g (3½oz) cooked wild rice

3 Tbsp finely chopped chives

1½ tsp salt

1 Tbsp caster sugar

1 tsp instant or fast-acting
dried yeast

Pour the cranberry juice into the bread pan first unless otherwise directed – some machines call for the yeast to be added first. Add the butter and half the white flour. Sprinkle over the rice flour, wild rice, chives, salt and sugar, and then the remaining white flour. Make a small indentation in the top and pile the yeast in the centre.

Fit the pan into the bread machine and set to the basic/normal setting, medium crust, 1-kg (2-lb) loaf size. Press Start.

When the bread is ready, carefully shake the loaf to remove it from the pan and transfer to a wire rack, standing the loaf the correct way up. Allow to cool for at least 1 hour before removing the kneading blade if necessary.

Rice flour gives a smooth, silky-textured crumb. I have added cooked wild rice – really an aquatic seed rather than a rice grain – and used cranberry juice as the liquid, which gives a pale pink bread. Toast lightly and top with cream cheese, smoked chicken and cranberry sauce.

Dark chocolate and walnut bread

Chocotastic {Makes 1 large loaf } Approx 800g/1lb 10oz

90g (3oz) very dark chocolate
(70% cocoa solids), broken
into small pieces
350ml (12fl oz) full-cream milk
30g (1oz) unsalted butter
450g (15oz) strong white bread flour
60g (2oz) walnut pieces, toasted
and chopped

1 tsp salt
2 Tbsp dark brown sugar
1 tsp instant or fast-acting
dried yeast
Egg white glaze (see page 25)
1 Tbsp vanilla sugar

Place the chocolate in a saucepan with the milk and butter. Heat very gently until melted and then allow to cool.

Pour the chocolate milk into the bread pan first unless otherwise directed – some machines call for the yeast to be added first. Add half the white flour and the walnuts. Sprinkle over the salt and sugar, and then add the remaining white flour. Make a small indentation in the top and pile the yeast in the centre.

Fit the pan into the bread machine and set to the basic/normal setting, medium crust, 1-kg (2-lb) loaf size. Press Start.

When the bread is ready, carefully shake the loaf to remove it from the pan and transfer to a wire rack, standing the loaf the correct way up. Immediately brush with the Egg white glaze and sprinkle with vanilla sugar. Allow to cool for at least 1 hour before removing the kneading blade if necessary.

I enjoy a double espresso mid-morning and I've found that this bread makes the perfect accompaniment. Try it on its own or, for an extra indulgent treat, spread with chocolate spread and a generous dollop of mascarpone or ricotta cheese. Omit the nuts if preferred.

86

Sweet spice and fruit loaf

Delicately perfumed {Makes 1 large loaf} Approx 800g/1lb 10oz

300ml (10fl oz) semi-skimmed milk

1 generous pinch saffron strands

1 vanilla pod, split

2 Tbsp runny honey

30g (1oz) unsalted butter

500g (1lb) soft-grain strong white bread flour

60g (2oz) no-soak dried apricots, finely chopped

60g (2oz) sultanas

1½ tsp salt

1 tsp instant or fast-acting dried yeast

Pour the milk into a saucepan and add the saffron and vanilla. Bring to just below boiling point and then remove from the heat and allow to infuse and cool. Remove the vanilla pod and stir in 1 tsp honey.

Pour the infused milk into the bread pan first unless otherwise directed – some machines call for the yeast to be added first. Add the butter and half the flour. Sprinkle over the apricots, sultanas, salt, 1 Tbsp honey and the remaining flour. Make a small indentation in the top and pile the yeast in the centre.

Fit the pan into the bread machine and set to the basic/normal setting, medium crust, 1-kg (2-lb) loaf size. Press Start.

When the bread is ready, carefully shake the loaf to remove it from the pan and transfer to a wire rack, standing the loaf the correct way up. Immediately brush the loaf with the remaining honey and allow to cool for at least 1 hour before removing the kneading blade if necessary.

This recipe includes two of my all-time favourite spices: saffron and vanilla, which also happen to be two of the most expensive! A loaf for special occasions, this is best served untoasted, spread with a little butter, soft cheese or honey and eaten with very little else; this way you'll be able to taste all the flavours.

Cardamom and candied fruit loaf

Fragrant {Makes 1 large loaf} Approx 950g/1lb 12oz

1 medium egg

About 250ml (8fl oz) semi-skimmed milk

100g (3½oz) marzipan, finely chopped

500g (1lb) strong white bread flour

100g (3½oz) candied fruit,

finely chopped

1½ tsp salt

3 cardamom pods, seeds removed

and ground

1 tsp instant or fast-acting

dried yeast

Beaten egg glaze (see page 24)

2 Tbsp flaked almonds, toasted

Beat the egg in a jug and add sufficient milk to make up to the 300ml (10fl oz) level then pour into the bread pan first unless otherwise directed – some machines call for the yeast to be added first. Add the marzipan and half the flour. Sprinkle over the fruit, salt, cardamom and then the remaining flour. Make a small indentation in the top and pile the yeast in the centre.

Fit the pan into the bread machine and set to the basic/normal setting, medium crust, 1-kg (2-lb) loaf size. Press Start.

When the bread is ready, carefully shake the loaf to remove it from the pan and transfer to a wire rack, standing the loaf the correct way up. Immediately brush with Beaten egg glaze and sprinkle with flaked almonds. Allow to cool for at least 1 hour before removing the kneading blade if necessary.

The flavours in this bread remind me of Christmas, and this loaf would certainly make a lighter alternative to the usual heavily fruited and rich festive fare. Good hot or cold, but best eaten within two days of baking while it is moist and fresh. Serve plain or buttered, with a glass of sherry, no other accompaniment required!

Coconut and date loaf

Tropical flavours {Makes 1 large loaf } Approx 1kg/2lb 2oz

350ml (12fl oz) coconut milk

2 tsp lime juice

2 medium eggs, beaten

500g (1lb) gluten-free white
bread flour

100g (3½oz) ripe mashed banana

60g (2oz) pitted unsweetened dates,
finely chopped

60g (2oz) unsweetened desiccated coconut

½ tsp salt

2 Tbsp + 1 tsp dark brown sugar

2 tsp instant or easy-blend
dried yeast

Pour the coconut milk, lime juice and eggs into the bread pan first unless otherwise directed – some machines call for the yeast to be added first. Add half the flour, banana, dates, coconut, salt and the sugar. Sprinkle over the remaining flour. Make a small indentation in the top and pile the yeast in the centre.

Fit the pan into the bread machine and set to the rapid or quick setting, medium crust, 1-kg (2-lb) loaf size. Press Start.

When the bread is ready, carefully shake the loaf to remove it from the pan and transfer to a wire rack, standing the loaf the correct way up. Allow to cool for at least 1 hour before removing the kneading blade if necessary. Best served warm.

A creamy-textured loaf with the natural sweetness of dried fruit and fresh banana. It is best served warm, and is lovely spread with ginger preserve or lime marmalade.

Apple pie bread

Home cooking {Makes 1 large loaf } Approx 1kg/2lb 2oz

350ml (12fl oz) unsweetened apple juice, at room temperature

30g (1oz) unsalted butter

500g (1lb) strong wholemeal bread flour

4 Tbsp apple sauce

60g (2oz) sultanas

1½ tsp salt

1 tsp ground cinnamon

¼ tsp ground nutmeg

1½ Tbsp light brown sugar

1 tsp instant or fast-acting dried yeast

Beaten egg glaze (see page 24)

Pour the apple juice into the bread pan first unless otherwise directed – some machines call for the yeast to be added first. Add the butter and half the flour. Add the apple sauce then sprinkle over the sultanas, salt, spices, sugar and the remaining flour. Make a small indentation in the top and pile the yeast in the centre.

Fit the pan into the bread machine and set to the whole wheat setting, medium crust, 1-kg (2-lb) loaf size. Press Start.

When the bread is ready, carefully shake the loaf to remove it from the pan and transfer to a wire rack, standing the loaf the correct way up. Immediately brush with the Beaten egg glaze and allow to cool for at least 1 hour before removing the kneading blade if necessary.

All the flavours you would expect to find in an apple pie captured in a tea-time loaf. Serve warm for the best flavour and texture, spread with clotted cream and a spoonful of jam or apple sauce.

Sour cherry and pecan rye loaf

New Yorker {Makes 1 large loaf } Approx 1kg/2lb 2oz

350ml (12fl oz) semi-skimmed milk

30g (1oz) unsalted butter

350g (12oz) strong white bread flour

150g (5oz) rye flour

1½ tsp salt

1½ Tbsp maple syrup

2 tsp lemon juice

60g (2oz) pecan halves, finely chopped

60g (2oz) stoned dried sour cherries, roughly chopped

1 tsp instant or fast-acting dried yeast

Pour the milk into the bread pan first unless otherwise directed – some machines call for the yeast to be added first. Add the butter and half of the flours. Sprinkle over the salt, maple syrup, lemon juice, pecans, cherries and then the remaining flour. Make a small indentation in the top and pile the yeast in the centre.

Fit the pan into the bread machine and set to the basic/normal setting, medium crust, 1-kg (2-lb) loaf size. Press Start.

When the bread is ready, carefully shake the loaf to remove it from the pan and transfer to a wire rack, standing the loaf the correct way up. Allow to cool for at least 1 hour before removing the kneading blade if necessary.

Inspired by the foods of America's most famous city, this loaf is not overly sweet so it is worth trying with some smoked ham or chicken piled on top. I prefer it with a dollop of crème fraîche or sour cream, more than a drizzle of maple syrup and some stoned fresh cherries...mmm!

Banana and chocolate chip bread

Fun {Makes 1 large loaf } Approx 1kg/2lb 2oz

300ml (10fl oz) semi-skimmed milk

30g (1oz) unsalted butter

500g (1lb) soft-grain strong
white bread flour

100g (3½oz) ripe mashed banana

100-g (3½-oz) packet plain
chocolate chips

1½ tsp salt

1 Tbsp light brown sugar

1 tsp instant or fast-acting
dried yeast

Pour the milk into the bread pan first unless otherwise directed – some machines call for the yeast to be added first. Add the butter and half the flour. Add the mashed banana then sprinkle over the chocolate chips, salt, sugar and the remaining flour. Make a small indentation in the top and pile the yeast in the centre.

Fit the pan into the bread machine and set to the basic/normal setting, medium crust, 1-kg (2-lb) loaf size. Press Start.

When the bread is ready, carefully shake the loaf to remove it from the pan and transfer to a wire rack, standing the loaf the correct way up. Allow to cool for at least 1 hour before removing the kneading blade if necessary.

This one is for the kids, really. It's ideal with Chocolate or Toffee spread (see page 178) or, for a healthier option, top with sliced banana and a little grated chocolate. I've used the soft-grain bread flour to increase the fibre content but you may prefer to use ordinary white bread flour.

If you use a ripe banana for this recipe, the natural sugar in the fruit will boost the sweetness of the finished loaf and also give a more intense banana flavour.

Doughs

100

Probably the most important and the most time-consuming stages of the bread-making process are the kneading and proving stages. If you don't want to end up elbow high in flour and dough or spend your time hanging around the kitchen wondering if the dough has had sufficient time to rise, then this is the time your bread machine "dough" programme comes into its own. Your bread machine will produce a silky smooth, glutenous dough which has proved to perfection. All you need to do is shape the dough, leave it to double in size in a warm place and then bake your bread in the oven!

Using the dough programme enables you to make different-shaped loaves from baguettes to flat breads, pizzas to bagels, and Danish pastries to savarin. You can finish your creations with a variety of different glazes and toppings to make them look glossy, seeded or softly floured. You'll be extending your bread-making skills and repertoire to that of a master baker before you reach the end of the chapter!

Focaccia with rosemary

Savoury {Makes 1 round loaf } 23cm/9in

200ml (7fl oz) water

100ml (3½fl oz) good-quality olive oil

450g (15oz) very strong white bread flour

1½ tsp salt

1½ tsp caster sugar

1 Tbsp finely chopped fresh rosemary or 1 tsp dried

2½ tsp instant or fast-acting dried yeast

Few sprigs fresh rosemary

Approx. 2 tsp coarse sea salt

Pour the water into the bread pan first unless otherwise directed – some machines call for the yeast to be added first. Add 75ml (3fl oz) oil. Sprinkle over half the flour and add the salt, sugar and chopped or dried rosemary. Sprinkle over the remaining flour and make a small indentation in the top and pile the yeast in the centre.

Fit the pan into the bread machine and set to the dough setting. Press Start.

When the cycle is complete, turn the dough on to a lightly floured surface and knead into a smooth, round ball. Press into a greased deep-sided

23-cm (9-in) round tin, lightly cover with a piece of oiled clingfilm and leave in a warm place for about 40 minutes until doubled in size. Preheat the oven to 200°C/400°F/Gas mark 6.

Lightly grease the end of the handle of a wooden spoon and press it into the top of the dough randomly to give the focaccia its traditional indented surface. Brush with some of the remaining oil, press small sprigs of rosemary into the top and sprinkle with sea salt to taste. Bake for about 30 minutes until golden, risen and the focaccia sounds hollow when tapped. Leave in the tin and transfer to a wire rack. Drizzle with the remaining oil and allow to cool. Best served warm.

An Italian round bread with indentations on the surface, richly flavoured and drizzled with olive oil. Serve warm and tear off pieces to eat.

Ciabatta

Airy {Makes 2 loaves } 350g/12oz each

300ml (10fl oz) sourdough starter (see page 13)
150ml (5fl oz) water
2 Tbsp good-quality olive oil
350g (12oz) strong white bread flour plus extra to dust

1½ tsp salt
¼ tsp instant or fast-acting dried yeast

Add the starter to the bread pan first unless otherwise directed – some machines call for the yeast to be added first. Pour in the water and oil. Sprinkle over the flour and salt. Make a small indentation in the top and pile the yeast in the centre. Set to the dough setting and press Start.

When the cycle is complete, turn the dough into a large oiled bowl (it will be quite soft and you will probably need to use a spatula) and cover loosely with oiled clingfilm. Leave to rise for about 1 hour 30 minutes until three times the size. Dust two large baking sheets with flour.

Using a sharp knife, cut the dough in half and place a piece on to each baking sheet. With floured hands, shape roughly into an oblong. Dust lightly with flour and set aside in a warm place for about 20 minutes to allow the dough to spread and rise. Preheat the oven to 200°C/400°F/Gas mark 6.

Bake in the oven for about 25 minutes until risen, golden and the ciabatta sounds hollow when tapped. Transfer to a wire rack to cool.

One of the most popular of all continental breads, this soft, flat-and-floury aerated Italian loaf is well known everywhere.

Brioche

Buttery {Makes 2 loaves } 450g/15oz each

8 Tbsp full-cream milk

3 large eggs, beaten

125ml (4fl oz) melted unsalted butter

2 Tbsp caster sugar

1 tsp salt

500g (1lb) strong white bread flour

2½ tsp instant or fast-acting
dried yeast

Egg yolk glaze (see page 24)

Pour the milk into the bread pan first unless otherwise directed – some machines call for the yeast to be added first. Add the eggs, melted butter, sugar and salt. Sprinkle over the flour. Make a small indentation in the top and pile the yeast in the centre.

Fit the pan into the bread machine and set to the dough setting. Press Start.

When the cycle is complete, turn the dough on to a lightly floured surface and knead into a smooth, round ball. Cut off a quarter of the dough and place in a bowl dusted with flour and cover with oiled clingfilm. Divide the remaining dough in two.

On a lightly floured surface, knead each piece of dough into a smooth round ball and place each into a greased 18-cm (7-in) diameter fluted brioche tin or a deep 16-cm (6½-in) round cake tin. Divide the remaining quarter of the dough in half and shape each into a small round. Place on top of each tin in the centre, and press down into the bottom ball of dough by pushing with a lightly greased wooden spoon handle. Cover loosely with lightly oiled clingfilm and leave in a warm place for about 40 minutes until well risen. Preheat the oven to 220°C/425°F/Gas mark 7.

Brush each brioche with Egg yolk glaze and bake for about 25 minutes until they are richly golden, well risen and sound hollow when tapped. Transfer to a wire rack to cool. Best served warm.

Instead of using the dough setting, choose the basic/normal setting and let the machine do the work for you (the loaf will then be bread-pan shaped!).

French bread

Traditional {Makes 2 baguettes } 350g/12oz each

325ml (11fl oz) water

500g (1lb) strong white bread flour

1 tsp caster sugar

1½ tsp salt

1½ tsp instant or fast-acting

dried yeast

Fine cornmeal or extra white

flour, to dust

Pour the water into the bread pan first unless otherwise directed – some machines call for the yeast to be added first. Sprinkle over the flour, sugar and salt. Make a small indentation in the top and pile the yeast in the centre.

Fit the pan into the bread machine and set to the French bread dough or dough setting (see introductory text above). Press Start.

When the cycle is complete, turn the dough on to a lightly floured surface and knead into a smooth, round ball. Divide into two equal pieces and form into long baguettes about 30cm (12in) long. Place on baking sheets dusted with cornmeal or flour. Set aside for 5 minutes.

Using a sharp knife, slash the tops with diagonal slits, and brush the tops with cold water. Place a roasting tray of boiling water in the bottom of a cold oven. Put the loaves in the oven and set the temperature to 200°C/400°F/ Gas mark 6. Bake the loaves for about 40 minutes until they are golden, crusty and sound hollow when tapped. Transfer to a wire rack to cool. Best served warm.

The combination of putting the loaves in a cold oven with a tray of hot water allows the loaves to prove and begin cooking in a steamy atmosphere, which helps set the texture and crust. Traditionally, French stick loaves are baked in floured bannetons – shallow, elongated tins which give the bread their familiar round shape. Bread baked on baking sheets will be flat-bottomed and more naturally shaped.

Pizza

Comfort food {Makes 2 round pizzas} 30cm/12in each to serve 6–8

1 quantity Simple white loaf dough (see page 32)

1 quantity Pizza sauce (see page 175)

2 quantities Pizza topping of your choice (see page 176)

Place the white bread dough ingredients in the bread machine pan as directed on page 32. Fit the pan into the bread machine and set to the dough setting. Press Start.

When the cycle is complete, turn the dough on to a lightly floured surface and knead into a smooth, round ball. Divide into two equal portions and fit into two 30-cm (12-in) lightly greased and floured round pizza tins. Alternatively, press free-form rounds on to greased baking sheets.

Spread with the Pizza sauce to within 2.5cm (1in) of the outside and cover with oiled clingfilm. Chill for 30 minutes.

Preheat the oven to 220°C/425°F/

Gas mark 7. Arrange the topping of your choice on top of the sauce and bake in the oven for 20–25 minutes until golden and cooked. Serve immediately, accompanied by a crisp salad.

One of my favourite snacks has got to be pizza. I like a thin, crispy crust with lots of topping. This recipe gives a medium crust – divide the dough accordingly to suit your preference.

English muffins

Tea-time treat {Makes 8}

150ml (5fl oz) full-cream milk

150ml (5fl oz) water

2 Tbsp melted unsalted butter

1 Tbsp caster sugar

1 tsp salt

250g (8oz) strong plain bread flour

250g (8oz) plain flour

2½ tsp instant or fast-acting dried yeast

Fine cornmeal or rice flour, to dust

Sunflower oil, for brushing

Pour the milk and water into the bread pan first unless otherwise directed – some machines call for the yeast to be added first. Add the butter, sugar and salt. Sprinkle over the flours. Make a small indentation in the top and pile the yeast in the centre.

Fit the pan into the bread machine and set to the dough setting. Press Start.

When the cycle is complete, turn the dough on to a lightly floured surface and knead into a smooth, round ball. Divide the dough into eight equal portions, and shape each into a round flat bun about 2cm (½in) thick. Dust each in a little cornmeal or rice flour all over. Place on a lightly floured tray and set in a warm place to prove for about 15 minutes, until they begin to lose their shape. Do not let them rise too much or they will become misshapen when cooking.

Heat a non-stick griddle or large frying pan over low to medium heat and brush with a little oil. Cook four–six muffins at a time, depending on the size of your pan for 8–10 minutes on each side, until golden on the top and bottom, but paler on the side. Take care not to over-brown too quickly as they will be doughy in the middle. Keep the remaining dough in the fridge to prevent over-proving. Wrap the cooked muffins in a clean tea towel or piece of muslin while you cook the remaining dough to keep them soft and prevent them drying out.

Best served warm, toasted or untoasted.

A traditional English tea-time treat. Served warm or toasted on both sides, the buns should never be cut apart, simply pulled apart. Serve filled or topped with a slice of butter or fill with strawberries and cream.

Almond danish pastries

Indulgent {Makes 8}

75ml (2½fl oz) full-cream milk

1 medium egg, beaten

30g (1oz) lard or white
vegetable fat

½ tsp salt

1 Tbsp caster sugar

275g (9oz) plain flour

1 tsp instant or fast-acting
dried yeast

90-g (3-oz) piece unsalted butter

125g (4oz) marzipan

Egg yolk glaze (see page 24)

30g (1oz) flaked almonds

Icing sugar, to dust

Pour the milk and egg into the bread pan first unless otherwise directed – some machines call for the yeast to be added first. Add the lard or white vegetable fat, the salt and sugar. Sprinkle over the flour. Make a small indentation in the top and pile the yeast in the centre.

Fit the pan into the bread machine and set to the dough setting. Press Start.

When the cycle is complete, turn the dough on to a lightly floured surface and knead into a smooth, round ball. Roll the dough out to form an oblong 38 x 15cm (15 x 6in) and place the piece of butter in the centre. Fold the dough over the butter, top and bottom, to cover it and press the edges to seal.

Turn the dough over and place squarely in front of you. Roll out gently to form an oblong the same size as directed above. Fold the top third down and the bottom third up, and turn 90 degrees. Cover and rest for

10 minutes. Repeat the rolling, folding, resting and turning twice more.

Roll out the dough into an oblong approx. 30 x 15cm (12 x 6 in), and cut into eight equal squares. Roll each to form a 10-cm (4-in) square. Place an eighth of the marzipan in the centre of each. Fold up the corners to cover the marzipan and secure with Egg yolk glaze. Arrange on a lightly floured large baking sheet, cover loosely with oiled clingfilm and leave in a warm place for about 20 minutes until doubled in size. Preheat the oven to 220°C/425°F/Gas mark 7.

Brush with Egg yolk glaze, sprinkle with flaked almonds and bake for about 15 minutes until golden and crisp. Transfer to a wire rack and cool. Best served warm, dusted with icing sugar.

Sweet spiced almond bread

Moorish {Makes 1 round loaf} 24cm/10in to serve 12

1 quantity Sweet spice and fruit loaf dough, made using strong white bread flour (see page 89)

200g (7oz) ground almonds

125g (4oz) caster sugar

4 green cardamom pods, seeds removed and ground

1 medium egg, beaten

1 tsp good quality vanilla extract

Egg white glaze (see page 24)

2 tsp icing sugar, to dust

Place the Sweet spice and fruit loaf dough ingredients in the bread machine pan as directed on page 89. Fit the pan into the bread machine and set to the dough setting. Press Start.

Meanwhile, mix the ground almonds with the caster sugar and ground cardamom. Bind together with the beaten egg and vanilla extract to form a smooth marzipan dough.

Cover and chill until required. Grease and line a 24-cm (10-in) spring clip cake tin.

When the cycle is complete, turn the dough on to a lightly floured surface and knead into a smooth, round ball. Roll the dough into a rectangle approximately 60 x 20cm (24 x 8in). Form the marzipan into a 2.5cm (1in) diameter sausage shape just shorter than the length of the dough and place the marzipan in the centre of the dough. Brush the edge of the dough with a little of the Egg white glaze and fold over to encase the marzipan, pressing the edges to seal well.

Coil the dough into the prepared tin, marzipan inwards, and cover loosely with oiled clingfilm. Set aside in a warm place for about an hour until risen. Preheat the oven to 200°C/400°F/

Gas mark 6. Brush the loaf with the remaining Egg white glaze and bake for about 30 minutes until richly golden. Cool in the tin for 10 minutes and then transfer to a wire rack. Best served warm, dusted with icing sugar.

Bagels

Deli-style {Makes 8}

250ml (8fl oz) water

2 Tbsp sunflower oil

2 Tbsp caster sugar

2 tsp salt

500g (1lb) strong plain white flour

2 tsp instant or fast-acting

dried yeast

Egg yolk glaze (see page 24)

2 Tbsp sesame or poppy seeds (optional)

Pour the water into the bread pan first unless otherwise directed – some machines call for the yeast to be added first. Add the oil, sugar and salt. Sprinkle over the flour. Make a small indentation in the top and pile the yeast in the centre.

Fit the pan into the bread machine and set to the dough setting. Press Start.

When the cycle is complete, turn the dough on to a lightly floured surface and knead into a smooth, round ball. Divide into eight equal pieces and shape each into a smooth round. Lightly grease the handle of a wooden spoon and press through the centre of each round, wiggling the spoon around to stretch and enlarge the hole.

Carefully transfer to an oiled baking sheet, spaced well apart, and cover with oiled clingfilm. Leave in a warm place for about 20 minutes until just starting to rise – take care not to leave them too long or they will become misshapen. Stretch open the central hole again if necessary.

Meanwhile, preheat the oven to 220°C/425°F/Gas mark 7. Bring a large shallow saucepan or deep-frying pan of water to the boil and reduce to a very gentle simmer. Poach two or three bagels in the water for 1 minute. Remove with a slotted spoon and place on a baking sheet lined with baking parchment. Poach and drain the remaining bagels.

Brush the bagels with Egg yolk glaze and sprinkle with seeds if using. Bake in the oven for about 15 minutes until richly golden. Transfer to a wire rack. Best served warm.

Doughnuts

Jammy {Makes 16}

250ml (8fl oz) semi-skimmed milk

2 large eggs, beaten

90g (3oz) unsalted butter, cut into small
pieces

½ tsp salt

1 Tbsp caster sugar, plus extra to dredge

500g (1lb) strong white bread flour

2½ tsp instant or fast-acting
dried yeast

125g (4oz) good-quality raspberry jam

Beaten egg glaze (see page 23)

Vegetable oil, for deep-frying

Pour the milk and eggs into the bread pan first unless otherwise directed – some machines call for the yeast to be added first. Add the small pieces of butter, salt and caster sugar. Sprinkle over the strong white bread flour. Make a small indentation in the top and pile the yeast in the centre.

Fit the pan into the bread machine and set to the dough setting. Press Start.

When the cycle is complete, turn the dough on to a lightly floured surface and knead into a smooth, round ball. Divide into 16 equal pieces then roll each piece into a round measuring about 7cm (3in).

Place a small spoonful of jam in the centre of each round and brush the edges with Beaten egg glaze. Pinch up the sides to encase the jam. Carefully shape each into a smooth, round bun. Transfer to an oiled baking sheet, cover with oiled clingfilm and set aside for 10 minutes.

Meanwhile, heat the oil for deep-frying in a large saucepan to 160°C/315°F. Cook the doughnuts in two batches for about 10 minutes, turning halfway through, until they are puffy and golden. Drain well on kitchen paper and dredge with extra caster sugar. Best served warm.

As children, we used to have doughnuts from the bakers once in a while for a treat, and I remember that we used to try and eat a whole doughnut without licking our lips to remove the sugar. It was quite a challenge, as I recall!

Flat breads

Middle Eastern {Makes 8} 100g/3½ oz each

300ml (10fl oz) water

4 Tbsp olive oil

1 tsp salt

1 tsp caster sugar

500g (1lb) strong white bread flour

1 tsp instant or fast-acting dried yeast

Pour the water into the bread pan first unless otherwise directed – some machines call for the yeast to be added first. Add 2 Tbsp oil, salt and sugar. Sprinkle over the flour. Make a small indentation in the top and pile the yeast in the centre.

Fit the pan into the bread machine and set to the dough setting. Press Start.

When the cycle is complete, turn the dough on to a lightly floured surface and knead into a smooth, round ball. Divide into eight equal pieces and roll each into a thin oval shape about 20.5cm (8 in) long. Transfer to greased baking sheets and cover with oiled clingfilm. Leave in a warm place for 20 minutes until just risen and slightly puffy. Preheat the oven to 220°C/425°F/Gas mark 7.

Brush each flat bread generously with the remaining olive oil and bake for about 10 minutes until puffy and golden. Best served warm.

These breads are better than any ready-made versions I have ever bought. They are quick to prepare and make a lunch or supper extra special. Good with dips for a light snack or as an accompaniment to salads or grilled meat dishes. You can sprinkle them with chopped garlic, dried herbs or seeds before baking if you like.

You can use wholemeal bread flour if you prefer, but you will need to increase the quantity of water to 350ml (12fl oz).

Naan

Takeaway {Makes 4} 200g/7oz each

200ml (7fl oz) water

100ml (3½fl oz) plain yogurt

1½ tsp salt

1 tsp caster sugar

1 tsp black onion seeds

4 Tbsp melted unsalted butter or ghee, plus extra to serve

500g (1lb) strong white bread flour

1¼ tsp instant or fast-acting dried yeast

Pour the water into the bread pan first unless otherwise directed – some machines call for the yeast to be added first. Add the yogurt, salt, sugar, onion seeds and butter or ghee. Sprinkle over the flour. Make a small indentation in the top and pile the yeast in the centre.

Fit the pan into the bread machine and set to the dough setting. Press Start.

Preheat the oven to the hottest setting, and place two large baking sheets in the oven. When the cycle is complete, turn the dough on to a lightly floured surface and knead into a smooth, round ball. Divide into four equal pieces and roll each piece out into an oval shape about 24cm (10in) long.

Carefully transfer the breads on to the preheated baking sheets and cook in the oven for about 6 minutes until puffed up. Meanwhile, preheat the grill to the hottest setting. Transfer the naans to the grill pan and continue to cook them for about 30 seconds on each side until they brown and blister – make sure they are not too close to the heat source or they will burn. Serve warm, brushed with extra melted butter or ghee.

Anyone who enjoys Indian food will no doubt be familiar with naan bread. These flat, leavened breads are traditionally cooked in a tandoor oven to give them a quick blast of dry heat that slightly chars the underside. It is possible to achieve a pretty good result without this type of oven, and I'm sure you'll be impressed.

Cinnamon pecan swirls

Favourite {Makes 12}

½ quantity Milk loaf dough
(see page 48)
90g (3oz) light brown sugar
60g (2oz) unsalted butter
100g (3½oz) pecans, finely chopped
1 tsp ground cinnamon

Vanilla-flavoured Glacé icing
(see page 24)

Add the bread dough ingredients to the pan as described on page 51. Fit the bread pan into the machine. Set to the dough setting and press Start.

Meanwhile, melt the sugar and butter together over low heat and stir in the pecans and cinnamon. Set aside to cool.

When the cycle is complete, turn the dough on to a lightly floured surface and knead into a smooth, round ball. Roll the dough to form an oblong 30 x 23cm (12 x 9 in). Break up the pecan paste and spread evenly over the whole surface of the dough. Roll the dough up tightly from one of the longest sides like a Swiss roll.

Cut the dough into 12 equal pieces and place side by side in a greased and lined 18 x 28-cm (7 x 11-in) rectangular cake tin. Cover with lightly oiled clingfilm and set aside in a warm place for about 1 hour until doubled in size.

Preheat the oven to 200°C/400°F/Gas mark 6. Bake the dough swirls for about 25 minutes until lightly golden. Cool for 10 minutes in the tin and then transfer to a wire rack.

Best served warm, drizzled with the glacé icing.

You can't beat one of these with a cup of freshly brewed coffee as a mid-morning treat. Soft white bread filled with a nutty, buttery layer – simply irresistible.

Grape, fig and cheese bread

Tuscan {Serves 8-10}

1 quantity plain Focaccia dough (see page 102)

350g (12oz) black grapes, washed, halved and pitted

3 ripe figs, thinly sliced

125g (4oz) no-soak dried figs, sliced

100g (3½oz) Italian blue cheese, e.g. Gorgonzola or Dolcelatte

1 Tbsp runny honey

Add the bread dough ingredients to the pan as described on page 102, omitting the rosemary. Fit the bread pan into the machine. Set to the dough setting and press Start.

When the cycle is complete, turn the dough on to a lightly floured surface and knead into a smooth, round ball. Cut in half and roll out half to form a circle measuring about 23cm (9 in). Place on a lightly oiled large baking sheet, and brush with some of the remaining olive oil.

Arrange the black grapes in the centre to within 2.5cm (1in) of the edge, and top with the fresh and dried figs. Crumble over the cheese. Roll out the other half of the dough, slightly larger than the first and place on top, pressing and sealing the edges well. Brush with more olive oil and, using a sharp knife, slash the top diagonally, to just reveal the filling. Cover with clingfilm and set aside for 20 minutes.

Preheat the oven to 200°C/400°F/Gas mark 6. Bake in the oven for about 30 minutes until richly golden. Brush with honey and cool for 15 minutes on the baking sheet then transfer to a wire rack. Best served warm, cut into wedges.

This is my version of a bread made in Italy to celebrate the Italian grape harvest. It's great served in place of dessert with a glass of port.

Hot cross buns

Easter choice {Makes 12}

300ml (10fl oz) full-cream milk

1 medium egg, beaten

60g (2oz) unsalted butter, melted

250g (8oz) strong white bread flour

½ tsp salt

60g (2oz) light brown sugar

2 tsp mixed spice

1 tsp finely grated orange rind

125g (4oz) currants

60g (2oz) sultanas

250g (8oz) strong wholemeal
bread flour

2 tsp instant or fast-acting dried yeast

To decorate

90g (3oz) plain flour

2 Tbsp vegetable oil

Beaten egg glaze (see page 23)

4 Tbsp full-cream milk

90g (3oz) caster sugar

Pour the milk into the bread pan first unless otherwise directed – some machines call for the yeast to be added first. Add the egg and melted butter. Sprinkle over the white flour. Add the salt, sugar, spice, orange rind, currants and sultanas and sprinkle over the wholemeal flour. Make a small indentation in the top and pile the yeast in the centre. Fit the pan into the bread machine and set to the dough setting. Press Start.

When the cycle is complete, turn the dough on to a lightly floured surface and knead into a smooth, round ball. Divide into 12 equal pieces and form each into a small, round ball. Place a little distance apart on a large greased baking sheet. Cover with oiled clingfilm and leave in a warm place for about 40 minutes until doubled in size.

Meanwhile, prepare the decoration. Mix the flour, oil and about 4 Tbsp water together to make a smooth, stiff paste. Place in a small piping bag with an opening about 6mm (¼in) in diameter. Preheat the oven to 220°C/425°F/Gas mark 7. Brush the buns with the Beaten egg glaze and pipe a cross on to each one. Bake for 15–20 minutes until golden.

Place 4 Tbsp milk in a saucepan with the caster sugar. Heat gently, stirring, until the sugar dissolves, bring to the boil and cook for 2 minutes. Once the buns are cooked, brush them with this glaze and transfer to a wire rack to cool.

Savarin

Sticky sweet {Serves 8-10}

100ml (3½fl oz) full-cream milk

4 medium eggs, beaten

100g (3½oz) unsalted butter, melted

½ tsp salt

2 Tbsp caster sugar

250g (8oz) strong white bread flour

1 tsp instant or fast-acting dried yeast

For the syrup

125g (4oz) granulated sugar

100ml (3½fl oz) water

1–2 tsp rosewater

To finish

150ml (5fl oz) whipping cream

1 tsp good-quality vanilla extract

180g (6oz) fresh raspberries and redcurrants

Pour the milk into the bread pan first unless otherwise directed – some machines call for the yeast to be added first. Add the eggs and melted butter. Add the salt and sugar, and sprinkle over the flour. Make a small indentation in the top and pile the yeast in the centre. Fit the pan into the bread machine and set to the dough setting. Press Start.

Turn the mixture (it will be very soft) into a lightly greased 1.5-L (30-fl oz) savarin or ring mould. Cover with oiled clingfilm and leave in a warm place for about 1 hour until the dough reaches the top of the tin. Preheat the oven to 200°C/ 400°F/Gas mark 6. Bake for about 25 minutes until golden and well risen. Transfer to a wire rack and place a plate underneath the rack, directly below the savarin. Allow to cool.

To make the syrup, place the sugar in a saucepan with the water and heat gently, stirring, until the sugar dissolves. Bring to the boil and cook for 2 minutes. Remove from the heat and cool for 10 minutes, then add the rosewater.

Spoon the hot syrup over the savarin, then spoon over the syrup that collects on the plate underneath. Transfer to a serving plate and allow to cool.

Lightly whip the cream with the vanilla extract until just peaking and pile into the centre of the savarin. Top with the raspberries and redcurrants, and serve.

Cakes and
breads

A bread machine can offer you more programmes than just ones for making bread or bread dough. Most models offer cake or dessert settings as well and their accompanying recipe books will give you suggestions for delicious bakes and sweet treats which can be mixed and cooked in the machine.

Traditional cakes and tea breads use baking powder rather than yeast as a raising agent, and they are usually slow-baked in the oven, giving them a light, moist texture. These types of bakes are also excellent cooked in your bread machine. You simply use the bread pan as your cake tin: grease and line it, and then fill it with the chosen mixture. Fix it into the machine and set the timer for cooking on the bake only setting.

I have included recipes for fruitcakes, tea loaves and a rich ginger cake, and there are also lighter cakes containing blueberries, pumpkin and ground nuts. There's even an incredibly rich chocolate cake! Once you get to know your machine it will be easy to adapt your own recipes and let the bread machine cook them for you.

Rich fruit cake

Festive {Serves 16}

500g (1lb) assorted dried fruits, e.g. currants, raisins, sultanas, chopped glacé cherries, chopped mixed peel and stem ginger pieces

100ml (3½fl oz) + 2 Tbsp dark rum

125g (4oz) unsalted butter, softened

125g (4oz) dark brown sugar

2 medium eggs, beaten

125g (4oz) plain flour

½ tsp salt

1½ tsp mixed spice

60g (2oz) flaked almonds

To decorate

1 Tbsp apricot jam, sieved

Icing sugar to dust

100g (3½oz) marzipan

150g (5oz) fondant icing

Christmas cake decorations

Place the assorted dried fruits in a large bowl and pour over 100ml (3½fl oz) rum. Mix well, cover and set aside for 2 hours to soak, stirring occasionally. Meanwhile, remove the kneading blade from the bread pan, and grease and line the bottom and sides with four layers of baking parchment.

In a large bowl, cream together the butter and sugar until light and creamy. Gradually beat in the eggs. Add the prepared dried fruit mixture and mix well. Sift in the flour, salt and spice and add the flaked almonds. Carefully fold in until well mixed.

Pile the mixture into the bread pan, making sure that the mixture is inside the parchment. Smooth the top.

Set the machine to the bake only setting, and enter 1 hour 15 minutes on the timer (see Note on page 20).

When the baking cycle is complete, test the cake by inserting a skewer into the centre: if it comes out clean, the cake is cooked. Select further time if necessary. If the skewer is only slightly sticky, the cake will continue to cook during the standing time.

Remove the pan from the machine and allow the cake to stand in the pan for 10 minutes. Carefully shake the cake to remove it from the pan and transfer to a wire rack, standing the cake the correct way up. Skewer the top in several places and spoon over the remaining rum. Allow to cool completely and discard the lining paper.

Wrap in greaseproof paper and foil, and store in a cool, dark place for a least 1 month and up to 1 year. Spoon over more rum every few weeks, if you like, to develop the cake's flavour and richness.

If you want to decorate the cake, brush the top of the cake with the apricot jam. Lightly dust the work surface with icing sugar and roll out the marzipan to fit the top of the cake, trimming as necessary.

Roll out the fondant icing to fit on top of the marzipan, trimming as necessary. Transfer to a cake board or serving plate.

Decorate with Christmas cake decorations and tie a length of ribbon around the cake, if using. Loosely wrap in greaseproof paper and store in a cool place for a day to allow the top to set.

To serve, remove the ribbon and cake decorations. Cut the cake in half lengthways and then each half into eight equal pieces.

If you prefer a less sweet topping, brush the top of the cake with jam or honey and arrange whole pieces of dried fruit and whole nuts in neat rows on top of the cake. Glaze with extra jam or honey if liked. Candied or glacé fruits also make a stunning contemporary topping.

Dark and squidgy ginger cake

Zingy {Makes 12 slices}

125g (4oz) treacle or molasses

125g (4oz) golden syrup

125g (4oz) dark brown sugar

125g (4oz) unsalted butter

250g (8oz) self-raising flour

½ tsp salt

1 tsp ground ginger

1 tsp mixed spice

60g (2oz) stem ginger, finely chopped

1 tsp finely grated orange rind

150ml (5fl oz) freshly squeezed orange juice

Remove the kneading blade from the bread pan, and grease and line the bottom and sides with baking parchment.

Place the treacle or molasses, syrup, sugar and butter in a saucepan and heat gently until melted together.

Sift the flour, salt, ground ginger and mixed spice into a bowl and make a well in the centre. Add the stem ginger, orange rind and orange juice. Pour in the melted treacle mixture, stirring to form a smooth, thick batter.

Pile the mixture into the bread pan, making sure that the mixture is inside the parchment. Smooth the top. Set the machine to the bake only setting, and enter 55 minutes on the timer (see Note on page 20).

When the baking cycle is complete, test the cake by inserting a skewer into the centre: if it comes out clean, the cake is cooked. If the skewer is only slightly sticky, the cake will continue to cook during the standing time. If the skewer is very sticky select further time.

Remove the pan from the machine and allow the cake to stand in the pan for 10 minutes. Carefully shake the cake to remove it from the pan and transfer to a wire rack, standing the cake the correct way up, and allow to cool.

Cut into slices to serve.

Spiced apple sauce cake

Saucy {Makes 8 thick slices}

250g (8oz) self-raising flour

1 tsp ground cinnamon

½ tsp salt

90g (3oz) unsalted butter

90g (3oz) light brown sugar

45g (1½oz) ground almonds

2 medium eggs, lightly beaten

6 Tbsp chunky apple sauce,

plus extra to serve

4 Tbsp full-cream milk

2 Tbsp demerara sugar

Remove the kneading blade from the bread pan, and grease and line the bottom and sides with baking parchment.

Sift the flour, cinnamon and salt into a bowl and rub in the butter until the mixture resembles fresh breadcrumbs. Stir in the light brown sugar and ground almonds. Gradually beat in the eggs and fold in the apple sauce and milk.

Pile the mixture into the bread pan, making sure that the mixture is inside the parchment. Smooth the top and sprinkle with demerara sugar. Set the machine to the bake only setting, and enter 50 minutes on the timer (see Note on page 20).

When the baking cycle is complete, test the cake by inserting a skewer into the centre: if it comes out clean, the cake is cooked. Select further time if necessary. If the skewer is only slightly sticky, the cake will continue to cook during the standing time.

Remove the pan from the machine and allow the cake to stand in the pan for 10 minutes. Carefully shake the cake to remove it from the pan and transfer to a wire rack, standing the cake the correct way up. Allow to cool.

To serve, cut into thick slices and serve with extra apple sauce.

You'll find this cake irresistible; it's moist and rich, with a hint of cinnamon, and is the perfect addition to the afternoon tea table. I could eat this anytime, though, and it is excellent with a mid-morning cup of coffee!

Very virtuous fruitcake

Too good to be true {Makes 10 slices}

250g (8oz) stoned dates,
roughly chopped

350ml (12fl oz) freshly squeezed orange
juice

165g (5½oz) spelt flour

60g (2oz) ground almonds

1 Tbsp baking powder

1 tsp mixed spice

250g (8oz) sultanas

250g (8oz) no-soak dried apricots,
finely chopped

1 tsp good-quality vanilla extract

Remove the kneading blade from the bread pan, and grease and line the bottom and sides with baking parchment.

Place the dates in a saucepan with the orange juice. Bring to the boil, then remove from the heat. Cool, then purée in a blender or food processor.

Place the flour in a bowl with the ground almonds, baking powder and spice. Stir in the sultanas and chopped apricots until well mixed, then stir in the date mixture and vanilla extract until well incorporated.

Pile the mixture into the bread pan, making sure that the mixture is inside the parchment. Smooth the top. Set the machine to the bake only setting, and enter 50 minutes on the timer (see Note on page 20).

When the baking cycle is complete, test the cake by inserting a skewer into the centre: if it comes out clean, the cake is cooked. Select further time if necessary. If the skewer is only slightly sticky, the cake will continue to cook during the standing time.

Remove the pan from the machine and allow the cake to stand in the pan for 10 minutes. Carefully shake the cake to remove it from the pan and transfer to a wire rack, standing the cake the correct way up, and allow to cool. Wrap well and keep for 24 hours before serving.

Cut into slices to serve.

A fantastic discovery! The mixture relies on natural sweetness from lots of dried fruit, but it has no fat or even eggs added to it. If you want to make it gluten-free, then you can use the flour of your choice.

Chocolate truffle cake

Decadent {Makes 10-12 slices}

200g (7oz) very dark chocolate
(70% cocoa solids)
125g (4oz) lightly salted butter
3 large eggs, separated
125g (4oz) dark brown sugar

3 Tbsp dark rum
1 tsp good-quality vanilla extract
150g (5oz) ground almonds
2 tsp baking powder

Remove the kneading blade from the bread pan, and grease and line the bottom and sides with baking parchment.

Break the chocolate into a heatproof bowl and add the butter. Melt over a saucepan of gently simmering water. Remove from the saucepan and allow to cool for 10 minutes.

Whisk the egg yolks and sugar together until pale, thick and creamy. In another bowl, whisk the egg whites until stiff.

Whisk the cooled chocolate, rum and vanilla into the egg and sugar mixture. Add the ground almonds, baking powder and egg whites. Carefully fold the dry ingredients into the chocolate mixture using a large metal spoon until well incorporated.

Pile the mixture into the bread pan, taking care that the mixture is inside the parchment. Smooth the top. Set the machine to the bake only setting, and enter 50 minutes on the timer (see Note on page 20).

When the baking cycle is complete, test the cake by inserting a skewer into the centre: if it comes out clean, the cake is cooked. Select further time if necessary. If the skewer is only slightly sticky, the cake will continue to cook during the standing time.

Remove the pan from the machine and allow the cake to stand in the pan for 10 minutes. Carefully shake the cake to remove it from the pan and transfer to a wire rack, standing the cake the correct way up, and allow to cool.

Cut into thin slices to serve.

Pumpkin and coconut loaf

Tropical {Makes 10 slices}

250g (8oz) pumpkin purée

4 Tbsp tinned coconut milk

1 large egg, beaten

180g (6oz) self-raising flour

½ tsp baking powder

½ tsp bicarbonate of soda

½ tsp ground nutmeg

½ tsp salt

60g (2oz) unsalted butter

150g (5oz) light brown sugar

4 Tbsp unsweetened desiccated coconut

Remove the kneading blade from the bread pan, and grease and line the bottom and sides with baking parchment.

In a bowl, mix the pumpkin purée with the coconut milk and egg. Sift the flour, baking powder, bicarbonate of soda, nutmeg and salt into another bowl, and rub in the butter until the mixture resembles fresh breadcrumbs. Stir in the sugar and coconut. Add the pumpkin purée mixture and mix well to form a thick batter.

Pour the mixture into the bread pan, making sure that the mixture is inside the parchment. Set the machine to the bake only setting, and enter 50 minutes on the timer (see Note on page 20).

When the baking cycle is complete, test the loaf by inserting a skewer into the centre: if it comes out clean, the loaf is cooked. Select further time if necessary. If the skewer is only slightly sticky, the loaf will continue to cook during the standing time.

Remove the pan from the machine and allow the loaf to stand in the pan for 10 minutes. Carefully shake the loaf to remove it from the pan and transfer to a wire rack, standing the loaf the correct way up, and allow to cool. Wrap well and keep for 24 hours before serving to allow the flavours to develop.

Cut into slices to serve.

Peanut butter tea-time loaf

Crunchy {Makes 10 slices}

150g (5oz) crunchy peanut butter

125g (4oz) light brown sugar

2 medium eggs, beaten

200ml (7fl oz) full-cream milk

1 tsp good-quality vanilla extract

400g (14oz) self-raising
wholemeal flour

Remove the kneading blade from the bread pan, and grease and line the bottom and sides with baking parchment.

Place the peanut butter in a bowl with the sugar. Beat together until light and creamy. Gradually beat in the eggs, milk and vanilla. Add the flour and stir into the peanut batter until smooth.

Pile the mixture into the bread pan, making sure that the mixture is inside the parchment. Set the machine to the bake only setting, and enter 45 minutes on the timer (see Note on page 20).

When the baking cycle is complete, test the loaf by inserting a skewer into the centre: if it comes out clean, the loaf is cooked. Select further time if necessary. If the skewer is only slightly sticky, the loaf will continue to cook during the standing time.

Remove the pan from the machine and allow the loaf to stand in the pan for 10 minutes. Carefully shake the loaf to remove it from the pan and transfer to a wire rack, standing the loaf the correct way up, and allow to cool.

Cut into slices to serve.

Fruity Earl Grey tea bread

Lemony {Makes 12 thin slices}

500g (1lb) currants
200g (7oz) light brown sugar
300ml (10fl oz) cold Earl Grey tea
1 medium egg, beaten
1 tsp finely grated lemon rind
275g (9oz) self-raising flour

Place the currants, sugar and Earl Grey in a bowl. Cover and leave to stand in a cool place for about 3 hours, until the currants have plumped up and softened.

Remove the kneading blade from the bread pan, and grease and line the bottom and sides with baking parchment.

Mix the egg and lemon rind into the soaked currants. Sift the flour over the fruit and carefully fold in until well incorporated.

Pile the mixture into the bread pan, making sure that the mixture is inside the parchment. Smooth the top. Set the machine to the bake only setting, and enter 1 hour 15 minutes on the timer (see Note on page 20).

When the baking cycle is complete, test the bread by inserting a skewer into the centre: if it comes out clean, the bread is cooked. Select further time if necessary. If the skewer is only slightly sticky, the bread will continue to cook during the standing time.

Remove the pan from the machine and allow the bread to stand in the pan for 10 minutes. Carefully shake the bread to remove it from the pan and transfer to a wire rack, standing the bread the correct way up, and allow to cool. Wrap well and keep for 24 hours before serving.

Cut into thin slices to serve.

Blueberry and pecan loaf

Berry ripe {Makes 10 slices}

250g (8oz) self-raising flour

½ tsp salt

125g (4oz) unsalted butter

125g (4oz) golden caster sugar

60g (2oz) ground pecan nuts

2 medium eggs, beaten

3 Tbsp full-cream milk

1 tsp good-quality vanilla extract

180g (6oz) fresh blueberries

30g (1oz) pecan nuts,

roughly chopped

Remove the kneading blade from the bread pan, and grease and line the bottom and sides with baking parchment.

Sift the flour and salt into a bowl and rub in the butter until the mixture resembles fresh breadcrumbs.

Stir in the sugar and ground pecans. Gradually beat in the eggs, milk and vanilla extract and fold in the blueberries.

Pile the mixture into the bread pan, making sure that the mixture is inside the parchment. Smooth the top and sprinkle with chopped pecans. Set the machine to the bake only setting, and enter 1 hour 10 minutes on the timer (see Note on page 20).

When the baking cycle is complete, test the loaf by inserting a skewer into the centre: if it comes out clean, the loaf is cooked. Select further time if necessary. If the skewer is only slightly sticky, the loaf will continue to cook during the standing time.

Remove the pan from the machine and allow the loaf to stand in the pan for 10 minutes. Carefully shake the loaf to remove it from the pan and transfer to a wire rack, standing the loaf the correct way up, and allow to cool.

Cut into slices to serve.

Plump, juicy blueberries and nutty pecans give this tea-time treat an American flavour. You can try other combinations such as raspberry and hazelnut or strawberry and almond.

Coffee and walnut loaf

Expresso {Makes 8 slices}

300g (10oz) plain flour

1 Tbsp baking powder

½ tsp salt

150g (5oz) light brown sugar

125g (4oz) finely chopped walnuts

2 Tbsp coffee essence

100ml (3½fl oz) full-cream milk

3 Tbsp melted unsalted butter

2 medium eggs, beaten

Glacé icing made with coffee

(see page 24) (optional)

Remove the kneading blade from the bread pan, and grease and line the bottom and sides with baking parchment.

Sift the flour, baking powder and salt into a bowl. Stir in the sugar and walnuts. Make a well in the centre and add the coffee essence, milk, melted butter and eggs, and gradually mix into the dry ingredients, until well incorporated.

Pile the mixture into the bread pan, making sure that the mixture is inside the parchment. Smooth the top. Set the machine to the bake only setting, and enter 50 minutes on the timer (see Note on page 20).

When the baking cycle is complete, test the loaf by inserting a skewer into the centre: if it comes out clean, the loaf is cooked. Select further time if necessary. If the skewer is only slightly sticky, the loaf will continue to cook during the standing time.

Remove the pan from the machine and allow the loaf to stand in the pan for 10 minutes. Carefully shake the loaf to remove it from the pan and transfer to a wire rack, standing the loaf the correct way up, and allow to cool. Drizzle with Glacé icing, if liked.

Cut into slices to serve.

A quick and easy bread that has a hint of sweetness. If you want to make it sweeter, make up a batch of Glacé icing (see page 24), using cold espresso or strong black coffee instead of water, and drizzle over the cake once it has cooled.

Serving
Suggestions

152

Apart from enjoying a thick slice of home-made bread on its own, bread is a versatile ingredient and can be used in a whole range of dishes. In this chapter, you'll find sweet and savoury recipes for using up leftover bread – even bread that is past its best freshness – and for making bread an integral part of a dish.

Taking a look through the following pages, you'll see that the recipes have a comforting appeal; some conjure up memories of childhood and family traditions, like Chocolate bread and butter pudding (see page 154) or Sweet berry basin pudding (see page 165), whilst others can provide a satisfying tasty snack with minimum effort – Croque monsieur (see page 166) or French toast (see page 163). If you have leftover dough, you can make bread sticks or pretzels, perfect for party nibbles or to serve with dips.

Once you've read through this book and started making your own bread you'll soon see that home-made bread is too good to waste, and I hope that I can inspire you to keep all those end crusts or the odd leftover slice in the freezer so you can use it in the future when you have the time to experiment.

Chocolate bread and butter pudding

Comforting {Serves 4-6}

90g (3oz) unsalted butter, softened

125g (4oz) no-soak dried prunes
or apricots, finely chopped

90g (3oz) very dark chocolate
(70% cocoa solids), grated

1 cinnamon stick, split in half

450ml (15fl oz) single cream

6 thick slices Dark chocolate and walnut bread (see
page 86)

3 medium eggs, beaten

2 Tbsp caster sugar

Preheat the oven to 180°C/350°F/Gas mark 4. Using a little of the butter, grease a
1.5-L (60-fl oz) ovenproof oval gratin dish. Sprinkle half the prunes or apricots on
the bottom of the dish. Set aside.

Place the chocolate, cinnamon stick and cream in a saucepan. Heat gently,
stirring, until just below boiling point – do not allow to boil – then remove from
the heat and leave to stand for 30 minutes.

Meanwhile, spread the bread thickly with the remaining butter and sandwich
two slices together; repeat for the other slices to make three sandwiches. Cut into
diagonal quarters and arrange, overlapping, in the prepared dish.

Whisk together the eggs and sugar until pale and frothy, and pour over the
chocolate milk straining it through a sieve. Mix well and then pour over the bread,
straining it again. Sprinkle with the remaining prunes or apricots.

Place the gratin dish in a roasting tin and pour sufficient water into the tin to
come halfway up the side of the dish. Bake for 40–45 minutes until the blade of
a knife inserted in the centre of the pudding comes out clean. Serve hot, with
pouring cream.

For a plain bread and butter pudding omit the chocolate and cinnamon from
the custard and add 1 tsp good-quality vanilla extract. Replace the prunes or
apricots with sultanas if preferred.

Queen of puddings

Traditional {Serves 4}

300ml (10fl oz) full-cream milk

60g (2oz) white breadcrumbs

Finely grated rind of 1 lemon

30g (1oz) unsalted butter

75g (2½oz) caster sugar

2 medium eggs, separated

2 Tbsp raspberry jam, softened

Thin strips of lemon rind, to decorate

To serve

Fresh raspberries

Pouring cream

Preheat the oven to 190°C/375°F/Gas mark 5. Heat the milk until just below boiling point. Place the breadcrumbs in a heatproof bowl and pour over the milk. Stir in the lemon rind, 15g (½oz) butter and 15g (½oz) sugar. Set aside for 30 minutes to soak.

Grease a 900-ml (30-fl oz) ovenproof gratin dish with the remaining butter. Mix the egg yolks into the breadcrumb mixture and spoon into the prepared dish. Smooth the top and bake for 30 minutes until just set. Reduce the oven temperature to 180°C/350°F/Gas mark 4.

Spread a thick layer of jam on top of the custard. Whisk the egg whites until very stiff and then fold in all but 1 Tbsp of the remaining sugar. Pile on top of the pudding, making sure all the custard is covered. Sprinkle with the remaining sugar. Bake for a further 20–25 minutes until the meringue is golden and crisp. Sprinkle with strips of lemon rind and serve immediately with fresh raspberries and pouring cream.

I was first introduced to this pudding in my cookery lessons at school, and it became a firm favourite. It has the winning combination of ingredients for me: bread, custard and meringue! It's an excellent way to use up leftover or stale bread and, in keeping with tradition, I'm using plain white breadcrumbs here.

Mediterranean bread terrine

Expresso {Makes 8 slices}

2 Tbsp finely grated fresh Parmesan cheese

13 slices bread about 1cm (½in) thick, e.g. Simple white loaf (see page 32), Simple wholemeal loaf (see page 35), Olive and pesto sourdough loaf (see page 55), crusts removed

6 Tbsp good-quality olive oil

4 Tbsp toasted pine nuts

4 Tbsp finely chopped basil

250g (8oz) mozzarella cheese, thinly sliced

1 quantity Pizza sauce (see page 177)

60g (2oz) stoned black olives in brine, drained and chopped

2 Tbsp fresh pesto sauce

Preheat the oven to 190°C/375°F/Gas mark 5. Grease and line a 30 x 11-cm (12 x 4 ½-in) loaf tin or terrine dish. Sprinkle the base with Parmesan.

Reserve four and a half slices of the bread. Brush one side of the remaining slices with oil and press into the tin or dish, slightly overlapping, curling slices round the corners, oiled side towards the tin sides, to fit snugly. Make sure the bottom and sides are completely covered – you should fit seven whole slices around the sides, and three half slices on the bottom. Sprinkle the bottom with half of the pine nuts, half of the basil and half of the mozzarella.

Make two of the reserved bread slices into fine breadcrumbs and mix into the Pizza sauce along with the olives. Pile into the centre of the tin, packing it down well. Top with the remaining pine nuts, basil and cheese. Finally spread over the pesto sauce.

Fit the remaining bread slices on top, overlapping slightly, gently pushing the bread down into the pesto sauce to make it fit securely. Brush with the remaining olive oil and place the tin on a baking sheet. Bake in the oven for about 1 hour, until richly golden brown. Cover the top with foil if necessary to prevent over-browning.

To serve, leave to stand for 10 minutes before removing from the tin or dish. Invert on to a serving board, slice with a bread knife and serve warm.

Caesar croûton salad

Crunchy {Serves 4}

4 slices white bread, crusts removed

60g (2oz) unsalted butter

6 Tbsp olive oil

2 cloves garlic, peeled

2 Tbsp finely grated fresh Parmesan cheese

2 Tbsp finely chopped chives

4 Little Gem lettuces,

trimmed and rinsed

60g (2oz) anchovy fillets in oil, drained

60g (2oz) stoned black olives in brine, drained

12 cherry tomatoes, halved

2 Tbsp single cream

Salt and freshly ground black pepper

1 tsp caster sugar

Cut the bread into small cubes. In a large frying pan, melt the butter with 4 Tbsp oil and 1 clove garlic – this will flavour the croûtons. When the butter is bubbling, stir, and add the croûtons. Keep the heat moderate, and stir the croûtons to ensure they all get coated in the butter mixture. They should start to crisp up and turn golden within about 2 minutes. Keep turning in the butter to make sure they are golden all over. Drain on kitchen paper and place in a heatproof dish. Discard the garlic clove.

Sprinkle the croûtons with the Parmesan and chives. Cover and keep warm.

When you are ready to serve, break up the lettuces and arrange in four shallow serving bowls. Roughly chop the anchovies and sprinkle a few over each portion. Add a few olives and cherry tomatoes.

Crush the remaining garlic clove and mix with the cream and remaining oil. Season and stir in the sugar. Drizzle a little over each salad. Sprinkle each salad with warm croûtons and serve immediately.

For croûton crumbs: cook the croûtons as above, omitting the garlic if preferred. Drain and allow to cool. Place in a blender or food processor and process for a few seconds until finely crushed. To serve, place the crumbs in a large frying pan and heat, stirring, for a few minutes until warm, taking care not to over-brown.

Grissini

Crisp {Makes 16 sticks} 25cm/10in each

½ batch Simple white loaf bread dough (see
page 32)
1 Tbsp good-quality olive oil
1 Tbsp fine cornmeal or polenta
Egg yolk glaze (see page 24)
1 Tbsp poppy seeds
1 Tbsp sesame seeds

Preheat the oven to 200°C/400°F/Gas mark 6. Divide the prepared dough into 16 equal pieces then roll and stretch the pieces into thin sticks about 25cm (10in) long on a lightly floured surface. Place on a large, lightly greased baking sheet.

Brush half the sticks with oil and sprinkle lightly with cornmeal or polenta. Brush the remaining sticks with Egg yolk glaze and sprinkle with poppy and sesame seeds. Bake in the oven for about 12 minutes until crisp and golden. Transfer to a wire rack and allow to cool. Delicious served warm or cold.

Flavour the dough by folding and kneading 1 Tbsp finely chopped fresh rosemary or 1 tsp dried into the finished dough before shaping.

You can make pretzels in the same way: divide the dough into 16 equal pieces and roll into lengths measuring about 25cm (10in). Form each into a pretzel shape by folding both ends inwards as though you were going to make a heart shape, but securing them nearer the base and forming two loops. Place on a large lightly greased baking sheet. Brush with Egg yolk glaze and sprinkle with poppy seeds and coarse salt. Bake and cool as for the grissini.

French toast

3 large eggs

2 Tbsp full-cream milk

1 pinch salt

4 thick slices bread, e.g. Simple white loaf (see
page 32), Simple wholemeal loaf (see page 35)
or Simple sourdough loaf (see page 52)

30g (1oz) unsalted butter

2 Tbsp sunflower oil

Lightly beat the eggs and milk together, and add salt. Pour on to a large plate. Lay
the slices of bread in the mixture, turning them to coat on both sides, and leave to
soak for 5 minutes.

Melt the butter with the oil in a large frying pan until frothy. Place the egg-
coated bread slices in the pan and spoon over any remaining beaten egg and milk
mixture. Cook over moderate heat for about 2 minutes until lightly golden. Turn
over and cook for a further 2 minutes until just set and golden. Drain and serve
warm with the accompaniment of your choice (see Tips below).

Serving suggestions:

Sprinkle with white sugar or drizzle with maple syrup and dust lightly with
grated nutmeg or ground cinnamon. Serve with poached apricots, fried
apple slices or fresh banana slices.

Season lightly with black pepper and a pinch of cayenne. Serve topped with
grilled bacon and sautéed mushrooms, and sprinkle with chopped parsley.

Add 4 Tbsp finely grated fresh Parmesan cheese to the beaten egg and cook
as above. Serve the bread with sliced fresh plum tomatoes and fresh basil.

Sage and onion stuffing

Traditional {Serves 4}

For the stuffing

1 Tbsp vegetable oil

1 large onion, finely chopped

180g (6oz) fresh white breadcrumbs

2 Tbsp finely chopped fresh sage
or 2 tsp dried

4 Tbsp melted butter

Salt and freshly ground black pepper

1 medium egg, beaten

Heat the oil in a frying pan and gently fry the onion for 5 minutes until softened but not browned. Transfer to a heatproof mixing bowl and stir in the remaining ingredients, seasoning well, and using the egg to bind the dry ingredients together. Cool slightly, then divide into eight portions and form each into a neat ball.

About 40 minutes before the roast poultry or game is cooked, spoon 3 Tbsp cooking juices into a small roasting tin and bake the stuffing balls alongside the bird for 30–35 minutes until golden and crisp. Drain and serve with the bird. If you want to cook the stuffing separately, set the oven to 190˚C/375˚F/Gas mark 5 and cook the stuffing balls in 3 Tbsp vegetable oil as above.

Nothing comes close to the comforting taste of homemade stuffing to accompany a roast chicken dinner.

Sweet berry basin pudding

Low fat and fruity {Serves 6}

8 large slices day-old white bread about 1cm
(½in) thick, crusts removed
900g (1lb 14oz) assorted prepared soft fruits,
e.g. raspberries, redcurrants, blackcurrants,
gooseberries and strawberries
About 125g (4oz) caster sugar

To serve
Clotted cream or créme fraîche

Reserve two slices of the bread and use the other slices to line the base and sides of a 900-ml (30-fl oz) pudding basin, trimming them to fit snugly, and ensuring that there are no gaps. Set aside.

Place all the fruit in a saucepan and add 2 Tbsp water and the sugar. Heat gently until the juices start to run, then increase the heat slightly and bring gently to the boil. Cover and simmer for about 3 minutes until the fruits are softened but still holding their shape. Remove from the heat and cool for 10 minutes. Taste and add more sugar if preferred.

Ladle the fruit and the cooking juices carefully into the bread-lined basin. Pack the fruit down firmly with the back of a spoon, but take care not to squash the fruit too much. Trim the remaining two slices of bread to fit the top and cover the fruit completely.

Lay a circle of baking parchment on the top and place a small flat plate on top of this. Weigh the plate down just on to the pudding surface with some heavy weights or a large tin. Refrigerate overnight to allow the juices to soak into the bread completely.

To serve, remove the weights, plate and parchment, and invert the pudding on to a flat serving plate. Shake lightly to remove the pudding from the basin. Cut into wedges and serve with clotted cream or créme fraîche.

Croque monsieur

Cheesy {Makes 1}

2 slices plain white bread about 1cm (½in) thick

60g (2oz) unsalted butter, softened

1 heaped tsp French mustard

2 Tbsp savoury white sauce

4 thin slices smoked ham

60g (2oz) Gruyére cheese, finely grated

Salt and freshly ground black pepper

2 Tbsp olive oil

Spread the bread with half the butter, and spread the mustard over one slice and the white sauce over the other. Top the sauced slice with ham and cheese and season well. Cover with the mustard-spread bread, and press down gently to make a sandwich.

Melt the remaining butter with the olive oil in a frying pan until frothy and cook the sandwich over moderate heat for about 2 minutes until golden. Turn over and cook for a further 2 minutes until golden and the cheese melts. Drain and serve immediately, cut in half diagonally.

A fried sandwich that really is worth the effort to make. Delicious served as a light lunch snack or supper dish with a glass of chilled French wine. Once you've got the basics, it's easy to ring the changes: experiment with different breads and cheeses or use smoked salmon or chicken instead of ham.

To make the savoury white sauce: in a jug, blend 1 Tbsp cornflour with a little milk to form a smooth paste. Top up to 200ml (7fl oz) with milk and mix well. Pour into a small saucepan and heat gently, stirring, until the sauce begins to boil then simmer for 1 minute. Season with a pinch of nutmeg and a little salt and pepper. Transfer to a small bowl and cover with a layer of clingfilm to prevent a skin forming. Allow to cool then cover and chill until required.

Hot chocolate, pear and marshmallow sandwich

Indulgent {Makes 1}

30g (1oz) unsalted butter, softened

2 slices bread about 1cm (½in) thick, e.g.

Simple white loaf (see page 32), Milk loaf (see

page 48) or Dark chocolate and walnut bread

(page 86)

2 Tbsp chocolate spread (page 178)

4 tinned pear halves in natural juice, drained

2 Tbsp mini marshmallows

To serve

Pouring cream (optional)

Thickly butter the bread and place buttered-side down on a board lined with baking parchment. Spread the unbuttered sides with chocolate spread.

Pat the pears dry using kitchen paper and slice thinly. Arrange over one slice of the bread and sprinkle with marshmallows. Peel the other slice of bread off the parchment and gently press, chocolate-side down, on top of the pears to make a sandwich.

Heat a non-stick ridged griddle or frying pan until hot, and press the sandwich on to the pan for about 2 minutes. Turn over and cook for a further 2 minutes until golden and lightly charred. Drain and serve immediately. Excellent with some pouring cream for extra indulgence!

If you're feeling a bit down in the dumps then this is the dish that could banish the blues and put you back on track. It contains all the ingredients to pick you up again: comforting bread, tender fruit, sweeties and, of course, chocolate. Use whatever bread you like but I think one of the sweeter recipes makes the best choice.

Mega club sandwich

Toastie {Makes 1}

3 slices Simple sourdough bread (see page 52)
about 1cm
(½in) thick
2 Tbsp olive oil
1 ripe vine tomato, thinly sliced
½ Little Gem lettuce, shredded
60g (2oz) smoked chicken breast, thinly sliced
2 rashers freshly grilled crispy bacon

2 Tbsp good-quality mayonnaise
1 Tbsp cranberry sauce
Freshly ground black pepper
2 cocktail gherkins

To serve
Salted crisps

Brush the bread on both sides with olive oil. Heat a non-stick ridged griddle or frying pan until hot, and press the bread slices on to the pan for about 2 minutes. Turn over and cook for a further 2 minutes until toasted and lightly charred.

As soon as the bread is toasted, layer two slices with tomato, lettuce, chicken and a rasher of bacon. Top each with a dollop of mayonnaise and cranberry sauce. Season well. Stack the two layers carefully on top of each other and press the remaining slice of bread on top. Secure each half of the bread with a short bamboo skewer and then slice in half diagonally.

Serve immediately, with a gherkin on each skewer, and with salted crisps as an accompaniment.

Traditionally a combination of three layers of toasted white bread filled with chicken, mayo, bacon and salad. Here I use griddled sourdough bread to give an altogether chunkier sandwich. You can use your favourite fillings, of course, and this is mine.

ACCOMPANIMENTS

Nut paste

Makes approx. 400g (14oz)

90g (3oz) unsalted roasted peanuts

90g (3oz) unsalted roasted cashew nuts

60g (2oz) pine nuts

30g (1oz) light brown sugar

1 tsp sea salt

100ml (3½fl oz) sunflower oil

Place all the ingredients in a blender or food processor and blend until smooth. Transfer to a sealable container and store in the refrigerator for up to 2 weeks. The mixture separates on standing, so mix well before using.

Toasted seed paste

Makes approx. 450g (15oz)

60g (2oz) sesame seeds

60g (2oz) sunflower seeds

60g (2oz) pumpkin seeds

½ tsp cumin seeds

30g (1oz) light brown sugar

1 tsp sea salt

150ml (5fl oz) sunflower oil

Place all the seeds in a large heavy-based pan and cook, stirring, over medium heat for 4–5 minutes until lightly toasted. Set aside to cool.

Place the seeds and the remaining ingredients in a blender or food processor and blend to form a crumbly paste. Transfer to a sealable container and store in the fridge for up to 2 weeks. The mixture separates on standing, so mix well before using

Hummus

Serves 4

410g (14oz) tin chickpeas,
drained and rinsed
½ clove garlic, crushed
1 Tbsp tahini (sesame seed paste)
3 Tbsp olive oil
2 Tbsp lemon juice
Salt and freshly ground black pepper

Place all the ingredients in a blender or food processor and blend until smooth and the consistency of softly whipped cream, adding a little water if necessary.

   Cover and chill until required, then serve dusted with paprika and a drizzle of olive oil.

Rarebit topping

Serves 2

15g (½oz) butter
15g (½oz) plain flour
1 tsp dry mustard
4 Tbsp stout or beer
1 dash Worcestershire sauce
250g (8oz) grated mature Cheddar cheese
Salt and freshly ground black pepper
2 slices toasted bread

Melt the butter in a small saucepan and blend in the flour and mustard.

Cook gently, stirring, for 1 minute. Blend in the stout or beer, and mix in the Worcestershire sauce, cheese and seasoning.

Pile on to the toasted bread and cook under a preheated medium grill for 2–3 minutes until golden and bubbling.

Instant beetroot chutney

Makes approx. 700g (1lb 7oz)

1 Tbsp sunflower oil

1 medium onion, finely chopped

1 clove garlic, crushed

1 tsp mixed pickling spice

2 Tbsp caster sugar

200ml (7fl oz) malt vinegar

2 Tbsp seedless raisins

400g (14oz) cooked beetroot in natural
juice, drained and grated

Salt and freshly ground black pepper

Heat the oil in a frying pan and gently fry the onion and garlic with the pickling spice for 10 minutes until just softened but not browned.

Add the sugar, vinegar and raisins and stir until the sugar dissolves. Bring to the boil and simmer for 10 minutes. Allow to cool then mix with the beetroot and seasoning. Spoon into a large jar and seal. Store in the fridge and use within 1 month

Pizza sauce

Makes sufficient for 2 x 30-cm (12-in) pizza bases

2 Tbsp olive oil

1 large onion, finely chopped

1 clove garlic, crushed

500g (1lb) tinned chopped tomatoes in rich

tomato juice

2 Tbsp tomato purée

1 tsp caster sugar

½ tsp salt

1 bay leaf

1 tsp dried oregano

Freshly ground black pepper

Heat the oil in a large saucepan and gently fry the onion and garlic for about 10 minutes until softened but not browned.

Stir in the remaining ingredients, bring to the boil and simmer for 20 minutes until thickened. Set aside to cool then discard the bay leaf. Cover and chill until required.

Pizza toppings

Each quantity is sufficient for 1 x 30-cm (12-in) pizza
See page 110 for assembling and cooking instructions

Tuna, anchovy, olive and caper
1 medium finely chopped red onion, 2 finely chopped cloves garlic, 200g (7oz) flaked tuna, 4 anchovy fillets, a handful of pitted black or green olives, 1–2 Tbsp drained capers. Sprinkle with 125g (4oz) grated mozzarella cheese and bake as directed. Once cooked, sprinkle with plenty of chopped parsley and black pepper before serving.

Four-cheese
60g (2oz) each of sliced mozzarella cheese, finely grated fresh Parmesan, crumbled Dolcelatte cheese and grated mature Cheddar cheese. Sprinkle with 1–2 tsp dried oregano and some black pepper before baking.

Chorizo and sun-dried tomato with avocado
125g (4oz) sliced chorizo sausage, 8 drained and chopped sun-dried tomatoes in oil. Sprinkle with 1–2 tsp hot smoked paprika before baking. Serve topped with sliced avocado and fresh coriander.

Rocket and Parmesan
Slice 4 ripe plum tomatoes thinly and spread over the top. Drizzle with 2 Tbsp olive oil and sprinkle with black pepper. Bake and serve piled high with wild rocket, fresh basil leaves and shavings of fresh Parmesan cheese.

All-day breakfast
Halve 4 thin pork sausages lengthwise through the middle and arrange on top. Add 4 chopped rashers unsmoked trimmed streaky bacon, 1 handful whole cherry tomatoes and 125g (4oz) sliced button mushrooms. Drizzle with a little olive oil and carefully break 2 small eggs on top. Season with black pepper and bake.

Lime and coconut curd

Makes approx. 650g (1lb 5oz)

4 limes
250g (8oz) caster sugar
125g (4oz) unsalted butter
2 large eggs + 1 large egg yolk
125g (4oz) coconut cream

Finely grate the green part of the lime rind, taking care not to include the bitter white pith. Halve the limes and extract 5 Tbsp juice.

Place the lime rind and juice in a heatproof bowl together with the sugar and butter. Stand the bowl over gently simmering water and stir until melted. Beat the eggs, egg yolk and coconut cream very well together. Strain through a nylon sieve into the lime mixture and stir until thickened enough to coat the back of a wooden spoon – this will take about 15 minutes. Spoon into hot, sterilised jars and seal. Store in the fridge for up to 1 month.

Chocolate spread

Makes 300g (10oz)

125g (4oz) milk or plain chocolate
60g (2oz) unsalted butter
3 Tbsp golden syrup
3 Tbsp double cream

Place all the ingredients in a saucepan and heat very gently, stirring, until melted together, then remove from the heat and allow to cool.

    Transfer to a sealable container and store in the fridge for up to 2 weeks.

Toffee spread

Makes 300g (10oz)

90g (3oz) unsalted butter
125g (4oz) light brown sugar
2 Tbsp golden syrup
4 Tbsp double cream

Place all the ingredients in a saucepan and heat very gently, stirring, until melted together and the sugar dissolves. Raise the heat and simmer for 2 minutes, then remove from the heat and allow to cool.

    Transfer to a sealable container and store in the fridge for up to 2 weeks.

Uncooked raspberry jam

Makes approx. 1kg (2lb)

500g (1lb) caster sugar
500g (1lb) fresh, ripe, unblemished raspberries, washed and patted dry

Preheat the oven to the lowest setting. Put the sugar in an ovenproof dish and place in the oven for about 15 minutes until just warm.

Put the raspberries in a bowl, add the sugar and mash together until the sugar has melted. Spoon into hot, sterilized jars, and seal well. Store unopened in the fridge for up to 1 month – once opened eat within 2 weeks.

Sandwich filling and topping suggestions

Each filling or topping is sufficient for 1 sandwich

Egg mayonnaise and watercress
Mash 2 cold, peeled medium hard-boiled eggs with 1½ Tbsp mayonnaise and ½ tsp English mustard. Season with black pepper. Spread over one slice of bread and top with plenty of fresh watercress, and sandwich together with another slice of bread.

Cheesy tuna and sweetcorn
Mix 125g (4oz) drained tinned tuna in brine with 1 Tbsp mayonnaise, 2 Tbsp cooked sweetcorn kernels and 60g (2oz) crumbled blue cheese. Pile on top of half a toasted baguette and cook under a medium preheated grill for 3–4 minutes until melted.

Curried chicken and mango chutney
Mix 125g (4oz) cooked skinless chopped chicken with 1 Tbsp mayonnaise, 1 Tbsp mango chutney and ½ tsp mild curry paste. Spread over one slice of bread and top with plenty of baby salad leaves. Sandwich together with another slice of bread.

Beef and horseradish
Mix 1 Tbsp mayonnaise with 1 tsp creamed horseradish sauce. Arrange 3 slices cooked roast beef on a slice of bread, and top with 1 handful wild rocket leaves, 2 slices of cooked beetroot and a few slices of red onion. Top with the horseradish mayonnaise, and sandwich together with another slice of bread.

Mixed vegetable salsa
Mix together 60g (2oz) grated carrot, 1 chopped spring onion, 4 chopped radishes and 2 Tbsp raisins with 2 Tbsp ready-made vinaigrette. Spread a slice of bread thickly with 3 Tbsp Hummus (see page 173) and pile the vegetables on top. Sandwich together with another slice of bread.

Sweet and sour chicken
Mix together ½ small chopped red pepper, 30g (1oz) tinned chopped pineapple, 1 chopped spring onion, 90g (3oz) finely chopped cooked skinless chicken and 2 Tbsp ready-made vinaigrette. Arrange a handful of shredded Chinese leaves over half a baguette and top with the chicken and vegetable mixture.

Italian roasted vegetables and salami
Mix together 30g (1oz) drained stoned chopped black olives in brine, 2 chopped sun-dried tomatoes in oil and 1 roasted and deseeded red pepper with 2 Tbsp ready-made vinaigrette. Arrange a few slices of Italian salami over a thick slice of toasted Ciabatta (see page 107) and pile the vegetables on top. Serve sprinkled with a few basil leaves.

Salmon tzaziki
Gently mix 125g (4oz) cold cooked flaked salmon with 2 Tbsp chopped cucumber, 1 tsp chopped red onion, 2 Tbsp plain yogurt and 1 tsp mint sauce. Line a slice of bread with shredded crisp lettuce and pile the salmon mixture on top. Serve as an open sandwich, sprinkled with a few mint leaves.

Fig and goat's cheese
Slice a large ripe fresh fig into six wedges. Spread 60g (2oz) soft, light-flavoured goat's cheese over a thick slice of bread and top with fig. Drizzle with clear honey.

Low fat ripe berry
Toast or griddle a thick slice of bread and serve spread with 45g (1½oz) low fat soft cheese. Top with a handful of assorted prepared ripe summer berries, such as small strawberries, raspberries, blueberries, etc., and drizzle with a little maple syrup.

Chocolate and banana
Lightly mash 1 ripe medium banana and pile on top of a thick slice of freshly toasted sweet bread. Sprinkle over 30g (1oz) crumbled flaked chocolate and top with a few fresh orange segments. Serve with a dollop of plain yogurt on top and a drizzle of maple syrup.

BIBLIOGRAPHY

Allison, Sonia, *The Complete Bread Machine Cookbook*, Ebury Press, 2001.

Davidson, Alan, *The Oxford Companion of Food*, Oxford University Press, 1999.

Leeming, Margaret, *A History of Food: From Manna to Microwave*, BBC Books, 1991.

Matthews, Wendy and Wells, Dilys, *Second Book of Food and Nutrition*, Home Economics and Domestic Subjects Review in association with the Flour Advisory Bureau, 1968.

McGee, Harold, *McGee On Food and Cooking*, Hodder & Stoughton, 2004.

Shapter, Jennie, *The Ultimate Bread Machine Cookbook*, Ted Smart, 2001.

Slater, Nigel, *Toast*, Fourth Estate, 2003.

Smith, Andrew, F, *The Oxford Encyclopedia of Food and Drink in America*, Oxford University Press 2004.

Stobart, Tom, *The Cook's Encyclopaedia*, Papermac, 1982.

Larousse Gastronomique, Paul Hamlyn, 1989.

ABOUT THE AUTHOR

Kathryn Hawkins is an experienced cookery writer and food stylist. She has worked on several women's magazines on the full-time staff and now as a freelancer. A former cookery editor of the bestselling weekly magazine *Woman's Own*, Kathryn moved to Scotland from London in 2004, and now works from her beautiful Victorian guesthouse overlooking Strathearn and the Ochil Hills. Kathryn enjoys using local produce in her cooking and writes on a wide range of cookery subjects. Her special interests include casual dining, regional food, cakes and baking, kid's cooking, food for health and healthy eating. Kathryn has been writing cookery books for over a decade and has written several books on healthy eating. She is a member of Guild of Food Writers and her ambition is to open and run her own cookery school.

GENERAL INDEX

almonds:
almond Danish pastries 114
chocolate truffle cake 141
sweet spiced almond bread 115
apples:
apple pie bread 93
spiced apple sauce cake 138
apricots:
sweet spice and fruit loaf 89
very virtuous fruitcake 139
ascorbic acid 16

bacon:
mega club sandwich 168
polenta bread with cheese
  and crispy bacon 78
bagels 116
baguettes (French bread) 109
baking powder 14
bananas: banana and
  chocolate chip bread 96
coconut and date loaf 92
beetroot: buckwheat, beetroot and
  caraway loaf 74
instant beetroot chutney 172
bicarbonate of soda 14
black bread 47
blueberries:
blueberry and pecan loaf 146
oatmeal and blueberry bread 67
Boston-style brown bread 58
bran 16
bread and butter pudding,
  chocolate 154

bread machines 18–23
bread making 8
ingredients 10–17
bread sticks (Grissini) 160
breakfast bread 64
brioche 106
brown bread flour 10
buckwheat flour 11
buckwheat, beetroot and caraway
  loaf 74
buns, hot cross 127
buttermilk:
Boston-style brown bread 58
oatmeal and blueberry bread 67

cakes and tea breads 130–49
cardamom: cardamom and candied
  fruit loaf 90
sweet spiced almond bread 115
carrot and cumin loaf 65
cheese 15
croque monsieur 166
grape, fig and cheese bread 124
Mediterranean bread terrine 157
polenta bread with cheese
  and crispy bacon 78
rarebit topping 173
three-cheese and tomato loaf 71
cherries:
sour cherry and pecan rye loaf 95
chicken:
mega club sandwich 168
chickpeas:
hummus 172

chillies:
sweet potato and chilli bread   82
chocolate   17
banana and chocolate
  chip bread   96
chocolate bread and
  butter pudding   154
chocolate spread   178
chocolate truffle cake   141
dark chocolate and walnut
  bread   86
hot chocolate, pear and
  marshmallow sandwich   167
Christmas cake (Rich fruit cake) 134–5
chutney, instant beetroot   174
ciabatta   105
cinnamon pecan swirls   123
club sandwich   168
coconut:
coconut and date loaf   92
lime and coconut curd   174
pumpkin and coconut loaf   142
sweet potato and chilli bread   84

coffee and walnut loaf   149
cornmeal   12
polenta bread with cheese and
  crispy bacon   78
smoky potato and corn bread   73
cranberry juice:
wild rice and cranberry loaf   85
croque monsieur   166
croûton salad Caesar-style   159
currants: Fruity Earl Grey
  tea bread   145
curried parsnip loaf   77

sour cherry and pecan rye loaf   95
sourdough starter   13
ciabatta   105
olive and pesto
  sourdough loaf   55
simple sourdough loaf   52
sweet onion sourdough loaf   56
soya flour   12
  protein-rich loaf   61
spelt flour   11
  breakfast bread   64
  spelt flour loaf   51
  very virtuous fruitcake   139
spiced apple sauce cake   138
spreads   170
storing dough and bread   24
strong white bread flour   10
stuffing, sage and onion   164
sugar   15
sultanas: apple pie bread   93
  very virtuous fruitcake   139
sweet berry basin pudding   165
sweet onion sourdough loaf   56
sweet potato and chilli bread   82
sweet rosemary bread   72
sweet spice and fruit loaf   89
sweet spiced almond bread   115
sweetcorn:
smoky potato and corn bread   73

tea: fruity Earl Grey tea bread   145
tea breads and cakes   130–49
terrine, Mediterranean bread   157
three-cheese and tomato loaf   71
toast, French   163
toasted nutty bread   44

toffee spread	178
tomatoes:	
nutty sun-dried tomato loaf	68
pizza sauce	172
three-cheese and	
tomato loaf	71
toppings	24
troubleshooting	26
very virtuous fruitcake	139
walnuts:	
coffee and walnut loaf	149
dark chocolate and	
walnut bread	88
wheat-based flours	10
wheatgerm	16
white bread flour	10
white loaf	32
wholemeal bread flour	10
wholemeal loaf	35
wild rice and cranberry loaf	85
xanthan gum	17
yeast	13, 25
yogurt:	
high-fibre loaf	62
smoky potato and corn bread	73

VEGETARIAN INDEX

almond Danish pastries 114
apple pie bread 93
bagels 116
banana and chocolate
  chip bread 96
black bread 47
blueberry and pecan loaf 146
Boston-style brown bread 58
breakfast bread 64
brioche 106
buckwheat, beetroot and
  caraway loaf 74
cardamom and candied
  fruit loaf 90
carrot and cumin loaf 68
chocolate bread and
  butter pudding 154
chocolate spread 178
chocolate truffle cake 141
ciabatta 105
cinnamon pecan swirls 123
coconut and date loaf 92
coffee and walnut loaf 149
curried parsnip loaf 77
dark and squidgy ginger cake 136
dark chocolate and
  walnut bread 86
darker rye loaf 43
doughnuts 118
English muffins 113
flat breads 119
focaccia with rosemary 102
French bread 109

French toast 163
fruity Earl Grey tea bread 145
grape, fig and cheese bread 124
grissini 160
high-fibre loaf 62
hot chocolate, pear and
  marshmallow sandwich 167
hot cross buns 127
hummus 172
instant beetroot chutney 174
light rye loaf 42
lime and coconut curd 177
malted grain loaf 39
Mediterranean bread terrine 157
milk loaf 48
naan 120
New England molasses bread 59
nut paste 170
nutty sun-dried tomato loaf 68
oatmeal and blueberry bread 67
olive and pesto sourdough loaf 55
peanut butter tea-time loaf 143
pizza 110
pizza sauce 175
protein-rich loaf 61
pumpkin and coconut loaf 142
queen of puddings 156
rarebit topping 173
rich fruitcake 134–5
sage and onion stuffing 164
savarin 128
seeded loaf 40
simple gluten-free loaf 45

simple sourdough loaf	52
simple white loaf	32
simple wholemeal loaf	35
smoky potato and corn bread	73
soft-grain bread	36
sour cherry and pecan rye loaf	95
spelt flour loaf	51
spiced apple sauce cake	138
sweet berry basin pudding	165
sweet onion sourdough loaf	56
sweet potato and chilli bread	82
sweet rosemary bread	72
sweet spice and fruit loaf	89
sweet spiced almond bread	115
three-cheese and tomato loaf	71
toasted nutty bread	44
toasted seed paste	171
toffee spread	178
uncooked raspberry jam	179
very virtuous fruitcake	139
wild rice and cranberry loaf	85

First published in Australia in 2010 by
New Holland Publishers (Australia) Pty Ltd
Sydney • Auckland • London • Cape Town
www.newholland.com.au
1/66 Gibbes Street Chatswood NSW 2067 Australia
218 Lake Road Northcote Auckland New Zealand
86 Edgware Road London W2 2EA United Kingdom
80 McKenzie Street Cape Town 8001 South Africa

A record of this book is available at the National Library of
Australia
ISBN 9781742570884

Senior Editor: Clare Hubbard
Editor: Anna Bennett
Designer: Amanda Tarlau
Photography: Stuart West
Home economy and food styling: Stella Murphy
Production: Hazel Kirkman
Editorial Direction: Rosemary Wilkinson
Production manager: Olga Dementiev

Printer: Toppan Leefung Printing Limited

ACKNOWLEDGEMENTS:
Thanks to Morphy Richards for giving us bread machines for
use for photography. For more information visit
www.morphyrichards.com.au or call 1300 002 756.